CULTURES OF THE WORLD
Chad

Cavendish
Square

New York

Published in 2021 by Cavendish Square Publishing, LLC
243 5th Avenue, Suite 136, New York, NY 10016
Copyright © 2021 by Cavendish Square Publishing, LLC

Third Edition

Website: cavendishsq.com

This publication represents the opinions and views of the author based on his or her personal experience, knowledge, and research. The information in this book serves as a general guide only. The author and publisher have used their best efforts in preparing this book and disclaim liability rising directly or indirectly from the use and application of this book.

All websites were available and accurate when this book was sent to press.

Library of Congress Cataloging-in-Publication Data

Names: Kneib, Martha, author. | Denton, Michelle, author.
Title: Chad / Martha Kneib and Michelle Denton.
Other titles: Cultures of the world (third edition)
Description: Third edition. | New York : Cavendish Square Publishing, 2021.
 | Series: Cultures of the world | Includes bibliographical references
 and index.
Identifiers: LCCN 2020053404 | ISBN 9781502662576 (library binding) | ISBN
 9781502662583 (ebook)
Subjects: LCSH: Chad--Juvenile literature.
Classification: LCC DT546.422 .K54 2021 | DDC 967.43--dc23
LC record available at https://lccn.loc.gov/2020053404

Writers: Martha Kneib; Michelle Denton, third edition
Editor, third edition: Michelle Denton
Designer, third edition: Jessica Nevins
Picture Researcher, third edition: Jessica Nevins

PICTURE CREDITS

CPSIA compliance information: Batch #CS22CSQ: For further information contact Cavendish Square Publishing LLC, New York, New York, at 1-877-980-4450.

Printed in the United States of America

Find us on

CONTENTS

CHAD TODAY

CHAD IS ONE OF THE LEAST-KNOWN COUNTRIES IN AFRICA, DESPITE having a rich history. Chad's location at the crossroads between the Sahara and Central Africa has made it a land where people have passed through, met, settled, and resettled for many centuries. Today, the presence of a large number of ethnic groups and languages contributes to the colorful fabric of Chadian history and makes it one of the most culturally diverse lands in the world. New income in the form of oil revenue has given a boost to the economy and is providing Chad a chance to expand its social and educational programs.

Fanning out from the eastern shores of Lake Chad, the country is large and made up mostly of desert. Being a desert nation, Chad struggles with food and water security. These problems are very concerning to humanitarian groups around the world. The remoteness of many villages is also an issue. Unreliable transportation systems make getting medical supplies such as medicine and vaccines to far-off groups a significant challenge.

Although effots to fix these problems have gone without government support for a long time, the people of Chad are ready and willing to help themselves and their

It is not uncommon to see active military members in cities in Chad because of terrorism in neighboring countries.

country. Organizations such as the United Nations (UN) hope that with proper support, Chad will flourish in the future.

CULTURE

There is no one culture in Chad. Chad is made up of the descendants of people from all over Africa and the Middle East, and each of these ethnic groups has their own unique culture. Many have maintained their ways of life for hundreds of years. Some live as nomadic or seminomadic cattle herders, living off the land as they travel to find food and water for their herds and their families. Sedentary people who live in cities and villages are generally farmers, and they grow sorghum, millet, corn, rice, and wheat, among other agricultural products.

Although the ways they live and express themselves may be different, the people of Chad do share some characteristics. Most live without access to electricity or running water, so life is kept simple and survival is key. However,

Chadians are known to be gracious hosts and very charitable to their neighbors. Food, especially, is often shared no matter how little of it there is. Family is considered the most important part of Chadian life, and people spend the majority of their time providing for their families even in the face of hardship.

In the Sahara, nomadic people ride camels across the sand.

GOVERNMENT CORRUPTION

Chad is considered a presidential republic, meaning that a democratically elected president leads the country as head of state. Idriss Déby, who has been president since 1990, has worked to bring international trade into Chad and keep terrorism from neighboring countries out. He has, in fact, set Chad up as a major force of antiterrorism peacekeeping in central Africa.

However, Chad is also considered one of the most corrupt countries in the world. Corruption, in a political sense, means that public power is being used for private gain. President Déby and his government have been repeatedly

caught misusing loans from other countries to buy weapons, and bribery is common throughout both the public and private sectors. Nepotism, or when powerful people put friends and family into jobs instead of qualified applicants, has made the government and the enforcement of laws very weak. The police are violent and often extort the people they are supposed to protect for money. Politicians who speak out against the corruption in Chad are fired, and newspapers that try to print the truth are generally intimidated into silence.

These realities make Chad a complicated country. The government's corruption touches every Chadian's life. Roads remain unpaved, supply chains remain spotty, and the people of Chad remain poor despite the economic growth brought by global trade.

THE OIL TRADE

Oil has only become Chad's biggest export in the last 20 years—before then it was cotton. Although Chad still produces cotton,

Idriss Déby, whose campaign poster here proclaims, "Together for an Emerging Chad," has been accused of rigging elections to stay in power.

the bulk of its gross domestic product (GDP) now comes from selling oil to global oil companies.

The oil project required the construction of a pipeline southwest through Cameroon to the coast, as well as the drilling of hundreds of oil wells across Chad. While some people have benefited from the new industry, most have not. Chad's local economy remains dependent on agriculture and animal herding, both of which have been deeply affected by the pipeline. People have lost fertile land for growing food, and animal pastures have been destroyed. Oil spills have also impacted Chad's fragile ecosystem. Animals such as lions, elephants, gazelles, and many species of birds, which were already struggling due to overhunting and climate change, are now also affected by the environmental fallout of oil production.

A LAND IN TURMOIL

Civil wars have peppered Chad's history. The country's diversity, although one of its strong points, is also a source of great conflict. When one group rises to power, the others have often been left behind or outright discriminated against. This tension continues to be seen within the government as different religious groups vie for power.

Chad has also been in conflict with its neighbors for many years. Previous fights with Sudan and Libya have kept tensions high in the region, and civil unrest in Sudan has sent hundreds of thousands of refugees fleeing into Chad. Recently, armed rebellion in Nigeria by the radical Islamist group Boko Haram has been keeping the Chadian military busy, and violent terrorist attacks have begun to escalate in Chad itself along the Nigerian border.

Even though the economy has begun growing, Chad remains an uncertain place. Environmental damage from the new oil industry and the effects of climate change have led to long droughts and the drying out of Lake Chad, the country's largest source of water. Preventable illnesses such as bacterial and parasitic diarrhea, hepatitis, and typhoid fever continue to ravage the population, and diseases such as malaria, dengue fever, and meningitis also remain common. Although the people of Chad have been through much turmoil in the form of droughts, wars, and diseases, they are emerging from these trials ready to embrace a more positive future.

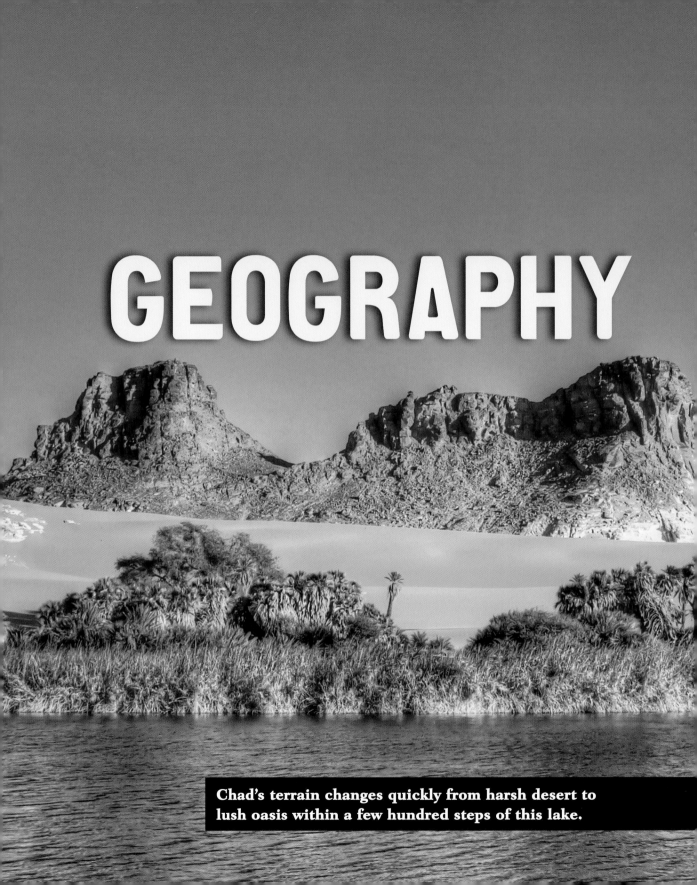

GEOGRAPHY

Chad's terrain changes quickly from harsh desert to lush oasis within a few hundred steps of this lake.

1

LOCATED IN NORTH-CENTRAL AFRICA, Chad stretches for 1,097 miles (1,765 kilometers) from north to south and averages 497 miles (800 km) from east to west. It covers a total of 495,755 square miles (1,284,000 sq km) and is roughly three times the size of California. Because of its size and location, Chad's geography varies almost as much as its culture, including both wide expanses of the Sahara to the north and the edge of a tropical zone to the south.

Chad is landlocked and bordered by six countries: Libya to the north, Sudan to the east, the Central African Republic to the south, and Niger, Nigeria, and Cameroon to the west. Because the country is landlocked, it has no ports. Its capital, N'Djamena, is more than 684 miles (1,100 km) from the Atlantic Ocean. An eastern city, Abéché, is around 1,647 miles (2,650 km) from the Red Sea, and a northern city, Faya-Largeau (sometimes referred to as Faya), is around 963 miles (1,550 km) from the Mediterranean Sea. Instead of relying on access to one of these major bodies of water, Chad unites around its namesake, Lake Chad, which sits along the western border.

GEOGRAPHIC ZONES

Chad boasts a wide variety of terrains, from deserts to tropical rain forests. It has mountains, plains, and deep basins containing interesting rock formations. This diversity has traditionally been divided into three geographical zones: Saharan, Sahelian, and Sudanian.

SAHARAN ZONE   The Saharan zone in northern Chad is a desert. It receives less than 8 inches (20 centimeters) of rain per year. This area supports few permanent settlements due to the lack of available water sources. As with all other deserts, the land gives up its heat quickly in the evening, leading to large temperature fluctuations between day and night.

This desert region is home to Chad's highest point, a volcanic peak called Emi Koussi, which is 11,204 feet (3,415 meters) above sea level. Emi Koussi is not only the highest point in the country, but also the highest in the Sahara. The lowest point in the country, the Djourab Depression, is also in this zone. It is 574 feet (175 m) above sea level and is in the northeastern part of the country.

The rugged area where Emi Koussi lies is along the Chadian-Libyan border. It is called the Tibesti Massif. A massif is an area of a mountain range independent of the rest of the range. The Tibesti Massif is made of very old rock separated from the other massifs to the east and the west by deep basins of younger rock. It contains areas of surface water in permanent pools, which are called gueltas. Gueltas are usually found in low points, such as ravines. This area also has seasonal watercourses. What little rainfall there is usually occurs between February and May.

The city of Faya lies within this desert zone. The town is situated at an oasis near the Tibesti Massif and is one of the largest oasis towns in the world, with a population of around 49,000 people. The town is surrounded by cliffs. Subterranean water makes agriculture possible near Faya, where wheat, dates, and figs are grown. Faya has been known to go more than a decade without significant rainfall. Because there are no paved roads in this area, those who wish to travel to Faya must use four-wheel-drive vehicles. The distance from the capital city, N'Djamena, to Faya is 589 miles (948 km).

North of Faya are the Lakes of Ounianga, a group of 18 lakes fed by groundwater that range from extremely salty to fresh enough to sustain plant and aquatic life. Several species of birds can also be found there, such as the desert lark, the desert sparrow, and the trumpeter finch. These lakes are the largest and deepest in the Sahara and are responsible for the human settlement of an area that receives less than an inch of rain annually.

Another town in the region is Fada, which has a population of more than 23,000 people. There are interesting rock formations around the town. The best-known geological formation is the Guelta d'Archei, a narrow red rock canyon that has been eroded over the ages into many fascinating towers and spikes. Deep in the canyon there are freshwater pools that are frequented by baboons. Fada is 560 miles (902 km) from the capital city.

SAHELIAN ZONE   The Sahelian zone of Chad encompasses the central portion of the country and contains the capital city and Lake Chad. This zone,

The Lakes of Ounianga create oases that are critical to the inhabitants of the Sahara.

The combination of wind and sand in the Ennedi plateau region has created fields of natural sculptures.

part of the semi-arid Sahel region of Africa, represents a transitional area between the Sahara to the north and the tropics to the south. Rainfall in the zone is highly irregular and is usually less than 20 inches (51 cm) per year. In 2010, severe drought in this area contributed to a food shortage that affected more than 2 million Chadians.

The northern part of the Sahelian zone is open grassland and thornbushes, while farther south is the savanna. The eastern part of the zone rises up to the remote Ennedi Massif. Over thousands of years, the sandstone mountain has been eroded into a plateau, and the highest point of the massif is only 4,757 feet (1,450 m) above sea level.

The Sahelian zone has a varied ecosystem. The arid thicket rat, which prefers lower elevations, is found in the region, as well as two endangered native gerbils, Burton's gerbil and Lowe's gerbil, which are found at higher elevations. Both gerbil species are considered critically endangered.

THE TOWERS OF ENNEDI

The Ennedi Massif, or Ennedi Plateau, is home to hundreds of towers, arches, and bridges carved from sandstone. Sandstone is a sedimentary rock composed of sand and held together by dry, compressed clay, and although it is of moderate hardness, it is easily eroded. These rock formations have been eroded by wind-blown sand over the years, but they were originally created by the tides of the ocean that covered the Sahara 550 to 250 million years ago. They range from 50 to 300 feet (15 to 91 m) tall, and many are free standing. The formations are generally only seen by nomads on camels as they move from one oasis to another, but a few brave tourists have traveled into the desert to climb them.

Mushroom-shaped towers such as this one are common on the Ennedi Plateau.

Larger animals, such as a desert antelope called the addax and several species of gazelle, such as the dama gazelle, dorcas gazelle, and red-fronted gazelle, also live in the Sahel. These animals are considered threatened or endangered. Until the 1980s, the scimitar oryx was found here, but it is now considered extinct in the wild.

Other animals that live in this region are the sand fox, a wild cat known as the caracal, the brown cape hare, the rock hyrax, and the desert hedgehog. These species are common.

Wildlife in the zone are well adapted to the dry climate in which they live. The dorcas gazelle, for instance, can acquire all the water it needs from the plants it eats.

The marabou stork is common in arid areas of Africa, including Chad. This stork is able to survive by eating scraps, dead animals, and even garbage.

The addax lives throughout the Saharan and Sahelian zones, but it is extremely rare in the wild due to unregulated hunting.

SUDANIAN ZONE   South of the Sahelian zone is the Sudanian zone. This region is dominated by a long dry season of 6 to 9 months and a rainy season when up to 24 inches (61 cm) of rain falls every year. The southern tip of Chad lies in a humid tropical zone, where more than 36 inches (91 cm) of rain falls every year. In this zone, the rainy season lasts six to nine months, and the dry season is short. Temperatures are high year-round, and the zone is mainly savanna with bushes and trees.

Wild animals are commonly found, partly due to reintroduction. Chad's Zakouma National Park is in the Sudanian zone. The park was opened in 1963, and it occupies 741,120 acres (299,920 hectares). During the dry season, visitors can see elephants, giraffes, lions, wildebeest, and many species of antelope. Due to the condition of the roads, traveling to the park, touring it, and getting back to the capital city can take six days.

Animal density in the park is higher than at many other parks in East Africa or South Africa, but park facilities and wildlife have been damaged by

the country's civil war. The park has not been able to attract as many tourists as its creators had hoped for.

Park animals are vulnerable to villagers nearby who kill them for food, so some effort has been made to involve the villagers in running the park. Most villagers live in poverty, and if they have other means of acquiring food to feed their families, such as earning money by taking care of the park, the park animals may face fewer threats.

Giraffes are native to southern Chad, and Zakouma National Park keeps more than 60 percent of the giraffe population safe.

WATER FEATURES

Chad has two permanent rivers. The Chari River flows for around 870 miles (1,400 km) and is formed from the tributaries of the Gribingui, Bamingui, Bahr Sara, and Bahr Salamat Rivers. The other river is the Logone River. This river flows for 240 miles (390 km) and is formed from the tributaries of the Pendé and M'Béré Rivers. The Logone River forms part of the border with Cameroon

North of Lake Chad are polders, or artificial lowlands protected by barriers called dikes. Floodwater is drained into the polders, and when it evaporates in the dry season, rich soil is left behind. The Yedina and Kotoko people who maintain the polders are able to raise two or sometimes three wheat crops each year. After 10 years, the polders are flooded for three years to regenerate the soil.

Due to the irregularity of the surface area of Lake Chad, the polders are only flooded during exceptionally rainy seasons, while during droughts only those closest to the lake will have water. The polders make approximately 150,000 acres (60,703 ha) of land available for agriculture, of which about half is being used at any one time.

and merges with the Chari River near N'Djamena. These rivers are navigable only during the rainy season.

The most important body of water that borders Chad, Niger, Nigeria, and Cameroon is Lake Chad. This lake occupied several hundred thousand square miles in prehistoric times when the area was much wetter, but it has since shrunk to a fraction of its former size. Ninety-five percent of the lake's water comes from the Chari River. During the rainy season, the lake may cover 9,843 square miles (25,493 sq km). During the dry season, it covers only 3,782 square miles (9,795 sq km).

Besides changing in size during the year, the lake may vary greatly from year to year. In 1870, the lake covered 10,808 square miles (27,993 sq km), but it had shrunk to 4,902 square miles (12,696 sq km) by 1908. The lake remained small until the end of the 1950s. After a wet period in the early 1960s, the lake regained most of its 1870 size, and by 1963, it covered 10,036 square miles (25,993 sq km).

Lake Chad is very shallow; in recent centuries, the lake has had a depth of less than 23 feet (7 m). Droughts during the 1970s and 1980s, however, caused the water level of the lake to drop to the point where, in 1984, it was possible to walk across it. In the future, increases in water demands by the four countries that border the lake may shrink it even further.

Chad has two other major lakes, Lake Fitri and Lake Iro. Lake Iro is in the southeastern region of the country in a marshy area. Lake Fitri, in the middle of the country, receives its water from seasonal watercourses, called wadis, in the northern region of the country that flow only during the rainy season. The northern part of the country has no permanent watercourses.

After the rains, the wadis are full of fish, which people catch and eat. The fish survive the dry seasons by burrowing deep in the mud and sleeping until the next time it rains. Although young men will brave the watercourses to catch fish, most people in the desert are afraid of water because flash floods are common and can, without warning, easily overcome and drown anyone in the wadi's channel. Such flash floods kill many people in desert areas around the world every year.

Chad is a large country with a small, unevenly distributed population that's centered on water. Most Chadians live in the south near Lake Chad and the country's two rivers.

REGIONS AND THE CAPITAL

Chad is composed of 23 regions. Within these 23 regions live more than 16 million people who belong to nearly 200 ethnic groups. Two of the main regions are Borkou and Chari-Baguirmi.

Covering 93,051 square miles (241,000 sq km), the Borkou region makes up almost half of the entire country of Chad. It is administered from Faya. Very few people live in this region, as it lies within the Sahara. Most of this region is extremely remote, and sandstorms constantly erase tracks and signs of truck routes. It can take up to two weeks for trucks to get from the capital city of N'Djamena to Faya.

Aouzou is a small town in the north of this region and was once a military outpost. The area where it is located, the Aouzou Strip, was occupied by Libyan forces in 1975, as it was believed that the area held deposits of uranium. During the 1980s, Chadian forces recovered much of the area, but it was not until 1994 that an international court determined that the entire region belonged to Chad. In May 1994, the UN's forces oversaw the withdrawal of the remaining Libyan troops.

N'Djamena is a low-lying city of concrete buildings and tin roofs, with architectural details influenced by the diverse groups of people who live there.

The Chari-Baguirmi region covers 17,761 square miles (46,001 sq km) and has an estimated population of nearly 621,800. The population of the region has doubled since the 1970s, mostly because it surrounds the Ville de N'Djamena region, the capital city.

Until April 6, 1973, N'Djamena was known as Fort Lamy. Its current name comes from the Arabic name of a nearby village, *Niǧāmīnā*, which means "place of rest." Its population is estimated to be around 721,000 people. Before 1984, conveniences such as electricity and water were either not present in the city or tightly rationed. Conditions have improved in the capital since that time.

Although N'Djamena still bears the scars of Chad's 30-year civil war, small signs of growth have appeared. The main street, Avenue du General de Gaulle, has several restaurants including a French restaurant and a Lebanese restaurant. The city has one museum, the Musée National, founded in 1962. The museum has displays documenting Chad's prehistory, paleontology, and ethnography. It also has an extensive collection of African art and is the home of the national archives.

A lack of basic services in the city remains. Many neighborhoods have taken it upon themselves to set up waste disposal services, since the city lacks an effective system of collecting and disposing refuse. Volunteers working in committees assemble donkey carts to haul trash out of the city to outlying dump sites. The committees have also built public restrooms. They originally had assistance from the UN Development Programme (UNDP) and are now raising funds for their work by selling waste containers.

INTERNET LINKS

www.africanparks.org/the-parks/zakouma
The African Parks website provides a detailed overview of Zakouma National Park, as well as information about its animals and community involvement.

www.africanworldheritagesites.org/natural-places/deserts/lakes-of-ounianga-chad.html
This web page features details and pictures of the Lakes of Ounianga, a World Heritage Site.

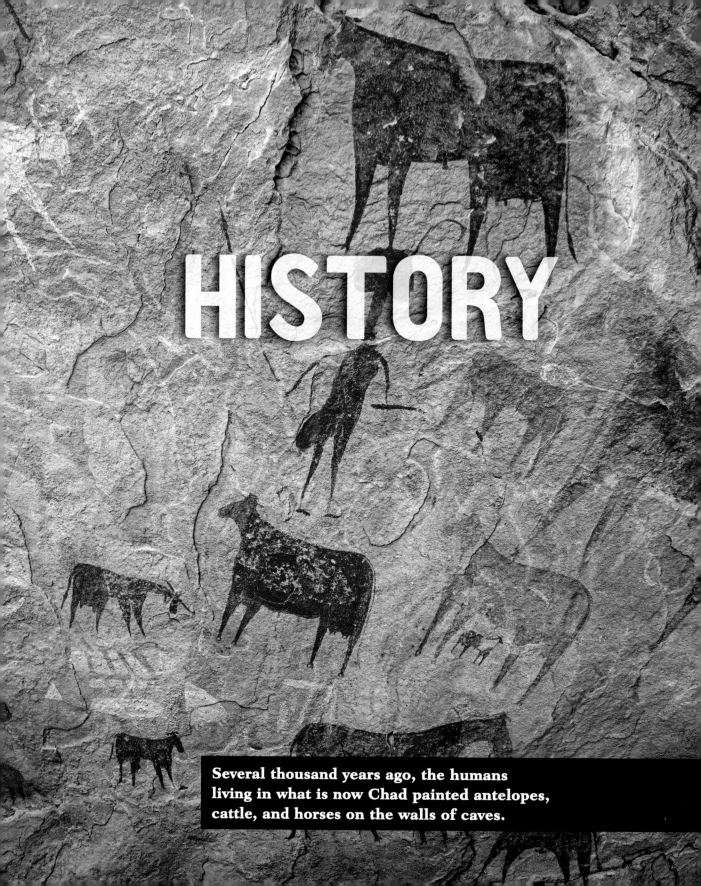

HISTORY

Several thousand years ago, the humans living in what is now Chad painted antelopes, cattle, and horses on the walls of caves.

2

THE HISTORY OF HABITATION IN Chad goes back to ancient times. In fact, scientists would argue that it even predates the evolution of modern humans. In 2002, anthropologists digging in the desert of northern Chad unearthed the skull of *Sahelanthropus tchadensis*, an African ape that lived approximately 7 million years ago. The skull was nicknamed Toumaï, a traditional name in the region for babies born before the dry season. Toumaï and its species lived around the time of the human-chimpanzee divergence, or the time when humans and chimpanzees last had a common ancestor, and they may have walked upright on two legs.

Modern humans have also lived in the area for quite a long time. Rock art paintings in the north of the country depict big-game animals such as antelopes in areas that are now desert. These paintings were made between 9,000 and 4,000 years ago, when the area was much wetter and had an abundance of wildlife.

Millions of years ago, Chad was home to many animals, including elephants, three-toed horses, giraffes, monkeys, and relatives of the hippopotamus called anthracotheriids.

Over thousands of years, the area dried out, but it remained a place of trade and migration routes. Two thousand years ago, during the Roman Empire, caravans passed through the area with goods bound for Rome. Throughout prehistoric and recorded history, the area that is now Chad has been an important and contended crossroads.

THE FIRST KINGDOM

Around the 11th century, several ethnic groups who lived in the northern area of what is now Chad formed a kingdom under the leadership of a group called the Zaghawa. The Zaghawa were made up of many families, and it was the Sayfawa family that established themselves as the ruling family. The Sayfawa dynasty ruled for centuries and was responsible for expanding the kingdom, named Kanem, into neighboring areas. By the 12th century, the kings of Kanem controlled many of the east-west and north-south caravan routes through the desert.

Traders brought Islam into the area, and the kings of Kanem converted from their native religion. Most of the local people, however, did not convert to Islam until around the 12th and 13th centuries, when the kingdom became large enough for great quantities of trade to come through. By that time, Kanem was an important route not only for trade but also for Muslim pilgrims on their way to Mecca.

Around 1380 CE, the Sayfawa lost their power and were exiled to a region called Borno, but they eventually regained their power over Kanem and founded what became known as the Kanem-Bornu Empire, which lasted for 500 years.

Famines in the 17th and 18th centuries began to undermine Sayfawa control of the empire. Invasions from nomadic groups such the Tuareg and the Fulani created insecurity. Bit by bit, Kanem-Bornu became smaller, and the rulers less powerful. In 1808, the empire's capital city was destroyed in a raid by the Fulani. The ruler moved the capital to a new location, but eventually the empire fell. Today, all that remains of the capital of the Kanem-Bornu Empire is ruins.

> *Alooma was the most celebrated ruler of Kanem-Bornu. Historians believe he reigned between 1570 and 1617 CE. An epic poem written about him tells of his victories in 1,000 battles. Alooma employed many military techniques new to the area: soldiers mounted on camels, walled military camps, permanent sieges, armored soldiers and horses, and musketeers trained by foreign military specialists. He also signed what is believed to be the first cease-fire in Chadian history.*

CONQUERORS FROM NEAR AND FAR

In 1883, Kanem-Bornu and its neighbors came under the control of a warlord and slave trader named Rābih az-Zubayr. Throughout the 1880s, Rābih conquered and expanded his control over the Kanem-Bornu kingdom and its neighbors. He then established his own capital in Dikwa, south of Lake Chad. However, he had made many enemies by defeating many powerful rulers. Some of them had heard about a new power in the area, the French. They allied themselves with the French in hopes of winning back their kingdoms.

In 1898, Rābih's forces fought several battles against an army of French and Bagirmi soldiers. As neither side would concede defeat, the fighting continued for two years. On April 22, 1900, when the two forces met at the Battle of Kousséri, the French forces defeated Rābih's army and killed him. Also killed was one of the French commanders, François Lamy. In his honor, the French named one of their outposts Fort Lamy, which today is Chad's capital, N'Djamena.

The French had a difficult time keeping peace in Chad. The extreme remoteness of the Chadian outposts meant that civil and military authorities had to travel long distances overland to get to their assignments. In 1928, about 45 percent of the civil-service positions were unfilled, as no one wanted to accept an assignment in Chad. To combat this, the French made arrangements with local chiefs, charging them to collect taxes and conscript labor. When this did not work, the French used excessive force to frighten the populace into obedience. Villages were depopulated, animals slaughtered or taken, and crops burned.

This drawing from 1860 shows Lake Chad before the French took over.

In order to make Chad a profitable holding, the French implemented forced labor on farmers to produce cotton. Women were recruited to work beside the men carrying dirt, cutting grass, and transporting stones, as well as cooking and fetching water for the rest of the laborers. Disease, starvation, and exhaustion killed many laborers. Some laborers were driven by hunger to raid nearby villages, thus spreading chaos and lawlessness. People deserted their villages to escape the raids. On some occasions, French administrators arrived at villages ready to conscript more labor only to find that everyone was already gone.

Others were taken to serve in the French army. During World War II (1939—1945), the French had an entire battalion composed of Chadians called the Régiment des Tirailleurs Sénégalais du Tchad, or the R.S.T. Casualties were high. Because service in the French army was so dangerous, violent resistance to recruitment was common.

The French also imposed taxes to be paid in cash on a population used to paying their chiefs taxes in kind. A man who raised cows gave a cow, for instance. The tax demands prompted more people to relocate to other areas. Such fugitives were pursued relentlessly. In general, French colonization led to economic disruption and population displacement in Chad.

In the 1920s, 20,000 Sara in the south of Chad, encouraged by their traditional leaders, refused to pay their taxes or provide any forced labor. Their local chiefs promised them that French bullets would turn to water rather than hurt them. Emboldened, the Sara rebelled against the French government. In response, the French killed 5,000 people, razed their villages, and slaughtered all the farm animals. Throughout their tenure in Chad, the French retaliated with excessive force against those who opposed their rule.

UNDER FRENCH COLONIALISM

French rule brought a few positive influences into the lives of the people of Chad. The French built schools and stopped the slave raiding of the south by the inhabitants of the north. The French presence was most strongly felt in the south, while in the Muslim north, the Arabs lived in relative autonomy. Though those in the south had to deal with a greater French presence, they also benefited from better access to education, health care, and positions of influence in the government. This led to resentment among northerners, who felt that their needs and concerns were not being adequately addressed. The southerners, meanwhile, kept alive their animosities toward northerners as a result of centuries of slave raiding. After Chad gained independence in 1960, this resentment continued unabated.

Northern and southern Chad were also divided by ethnicity, lifestyle, and religion. In the north, the population was made up of Arabs and groups such as the Toubou. Most practiced Islam, and as the region had little permanent water or arable land, most people were nomadic herders. In the south, the Sara were the dominant ethnic group. They were farmers and followed native religions or Christianity. The French called the south *Tchad utile*, or "useful Chad." The north was *Tchad inutile*, "useless Chad," and it contributed little to the economy.

The French outlawed native languages, fearing that Chadians would plan revolts in languages the French did not understand. The mandatory use of French left a legacy in Chad: Today, many people have French names such as Souffrance (Suffering), Tristesse (Sadness), and Douleur (Pain).

After World War II, the French abolished forced labor and made all Chadians French citizens. In 1945, political parties were permitted for the first time. Chadians elected delegates to the French National Assembly, and in 1952 to the Territorial Assembly. Both men and women were allowed to vote, and people of all races and ethnic groups voted in the same places.

One of the best-known political groups of the time was the Union Démocratique Tchadienne (UDT), founded in 1947. It was concerned mainly with Muslim interests and therefore was more popular in the north. To achieve their goals, members of this political party cooperated with parties founded by French people living in Chad.

Parties in the south, such as the Parti Progressiste Tchadien (PPT), were more interested in ending forced cotton production and the French rule. Parties such as the PPT did not seek to cooperate with the French and so were viewed with suspicion by the authorities.

The political situation was chaotic during this time. Chadians sought political parties that would, for the first time, represent their own interests rather than the interests of a king or the French, but the result was dozens of parties being formed, each responsible only to a small, core group. A confusing array of parties battled each other for seats in the Territorial Assembly at every election. The PPT, though, began to emerge as a strong party in the north as well as the south.

Despite problems and occasional violence, the first predominantly native government in Chad was formed in 1958. The PPT was in power, but not for long. Within four months, the government had been disbanded and reformed four times under opposition pressure. Finally, on June 16, 1959, the PPT, under the leadership of François Tombalbaye, emerged triumphant.

INDEPENDENT CHAD

Chad gained its independence from France on August 11, 1960. Tombalbaye, who was from the south of the country, led the country from that point until 1975. His regime was noted for promoting southern domination over other regions of the country.

Tombalbaye was the country's first president as well as the leader of its armed forces. He appointed all members of the Supreme Court, all provincial governors (prefects), and his cabinet. The country had a National Assembly, but it existed merely to rubber-stamp the president's decisions. Opponents to Tombalbaye's regime were removed from their positions. Some were arrested and sent to prison.

In 1963, during an antigovernment protest, 500 Chadians were killed. Tombalbaye declared a state of emergency. Under these conditions, northern Chad grew increasingly restless. Leaders in the south were also unhappy with Tombalbaye, but as he favored them over the north, they grumbled less.

In 1968, Tombalbaye launched his "Cultural Revolution" designed to rid Chad of foreign influences and colonial practices. Street names were changed, and the capital, Fort Lamy, was renamed N'Djamena in April 1973. All government officials were required to change their French names to traditional African ones. Tombalbaye himself dropped his first name, François, in favor of N'Garta, which means "chief." On the street, people were encouraged to greet each other as *compatriote* rather than *Monsieur*.

Some requirements of the "Cultural Revolution" outraged even Tombalbaye's supporters. He ordered the return of a traditional Sara initiation rite, yondo, which involved circumcision. During the 20th century, yondo rites had largely been abandoned, especially by those who had converted to Christianity. Now government workers who had not been initiated, even those in their 50s, were forced to undergo the rites.

Tombalbaye also arrested dozens of people, including some from his own PPT party, whom he accused of using voodoo magic against him. He weakened the army, brought in foreign advisers for his own security, and hired Moroccan bodyguards. He sometimes boasted he had survived more assassination attempts than any other African leader.

Opponents to these changes, many of whom were southerners, were exiled, arrested, beaten to death, or burned alive. Increasingly, southern voices were raised with northern ones in opposition to Tombalbaye's government. On April 13, 1975, junior officers of the army along with other military personnel launched a coup and killed Tombalbaye.

In 1976, President Malloum (*seated, right*) hosted French prime minister Jacques Chirac (*seated, left*), and the two signed agreements to strengthen military cooperation between their countries.

CIVIL WAR AND FOREIGN TENSIONS

General Félix Malloum became the next president of Chad. He tried to stem the tide of resentment against the government by appointing Muslims to his cabinet and freeing political prisoners. Some rebel groups reconciled with the government, but some, including those led by Toubou leader Hissène Habré, did not. By 1976, Malloum had become the target of assassination attempts.

Violence in Chad continued unabated. During several battles with rebels, nearly 2,000 Chadian soldiers died. To try to stop further rebellion and deaths, Malloum appointed Habré as prime minister in August 1978. The two men had vastly different agendas, however, and could not work together. In February 1979, civil war broke out.

By 1982, Habré managed to wrest control over the whole of Chad. Coincidentally, several years of heavy rains brought abundant harvests, and the populace was better fed than it had been in some time. This helped bolster Habré's position. The completion of a bridge across the Logone River, which linked N'Djamena with Kousséri in Cameroon, eased transportation problems. Goods could now be shipped out of the country more easily. Schools were full of children, and the international community began paying more attention to what was happening in Chad.

Habré's tenure as leader of the country was marked by a national army that was better trained and more disciplined than before. It also marked the end of Chad's isolation from much of the outside world.

In 1990, however, one of Habré's former supporters, Idriss Déby, gathered a rebel army and captured N'Djamena. Habré fled the country. He was arrested in Senegal in 2013 and put on trial for torture and crimes against humanity in 2015. Rights groups claimed that 40,000 people had been killed under his rule. In 2016, he was found guilty and sentenced to life in prison.

Hissène Habré, shown here in 1983, brought Chad to the world stage but was cruel and uncompromising to maintain his powerful position.

Idriss Déby has worked hard to protect Chad against terrorism, but his four re-elections have cast doubt on the legitimacy of his government.

Déby tried to re-create a multiparty political system in Chad, and by 1993, there were 26 political parties. In 1996, 2001, 2006, 2011, and 2016, Déby was elected president.

Déby's former defense minister, Youssouf Togoimi, began a rebellion against Déby's government in 1998. They signed a cease-fire in January 2002. In 2003, another rebel group in the southeast, the National Resistance Army, agreed to a cease-fire. Despite the official agreements to put down their weapons, not all rebels have done so, especially in the north, which is strewn with many land mines. In April 2006, rebel forces entered N'Djamena in an effort to overthrow President Déby. However, government troops fought back with President Déby declaring, "The situation is under control."

During these years, tensions with neighboring Sudan began to rise. A radical Islamist movement within the country sent thousands of Sudanese refugees fleeing into Chad, and violence spilled over Chad's eastern border. The 2006 attempt to overthrow Déby was blamed on Sudan, and it was then that Chad officially cut diplomatic ties with its neighbor. It took four years and much bloodshed before the conflict came to a close.

In recent years, Chad has distinguished itself as an oil producer and antiterrorism force. It is clear that Chad has stepped into a peacekeeping role within the region, aligning itself with the UN to help countries, such as Mali, facing political unrest. In 2020, President Déby even abolished the death penalty. Unfortunately, corruption within Déby's government has cast a shadow over these accomplishments. With journalists, trade unionists, and political opponents routinely silenced and the validity of elections called into question, many would call President Déby a dictator. A new constitution, which expanded the president's powers, was passed in 2018.

INTERNET LINKS

www.ancient.eu/Kingdom_of_Kanem/
This web page from the Ancient History Encyclopedia details the history and cultural impact of the Kanem-Bornu Empire.

www.bbc.com/news/world-africa-13164690
This article from the BBC includes a comprehensive timeline of Chad's history.

GOVERNMENT

The Chadian flag has three vertical stripes of blue, gold, and red, which symbolize hope, the sun, and national unity.

• • • • • • • • • • • • • • •
"A tyrant is only a
slave turned
inside out."
—Chadian proverb

DRISS DÉBY TOOK OVER THE administration of Chad in December 1990 and promised to promote freedom, justice, and multiparty democracy. However, it soon became clear that he was in no hurry to fulfill this promise. In 1992, the French withdrew their air-strike force from Chad. Many people believed this was France's way of telling Déby that French support for his administration rested on him holding elections in Chad.

In January 1993, Déby opened a conference, called the Sovereign National Conference, that was supposed to draw up a new constitution for Chad. The conference appointed an interim government, led by Déby, that was supposed to last for one year. It lasted for three years, but finally, in 1996, Chad had a new constitution and held presidential elections. Elections were held every five years after that, with President Déby being reelected each time.

The 2018 constitution, in addition to expanding the president's powers, eliminated the position of prime minister, giving Déby sole control as head of state. Opponent lawmakers, who boycotted the vote to approve the new constitution, said that this was a move meant to install a kind of monarchy. Although the constitution now sets a two-term limit on the president, it did not go into effect retroactively, meaning Déby still has two terms ahead of him, which were extended to six years in length.

HOW THE GOVERNMENT WORKS

The government of Chad is headed by a president. Since 1990, the president of Chad has been Idriss Déby. The president appoints his cabinet and also helps to decide on appointments for positions on the Supreme Court, other judicial openings, generals, and provincial officials.

The president must be elected by more than 50 percent of the popular vote and is elected to a six-year term. If no one receives 50 percent of the vote, the two candidates who have the most votes stand in a second round of voting.

The National Assembly, which has 155 members elected by popular vote to four-year terms, is the main body of the legislative branch of the government. The National Assembly meets twice a year, in March and October. Special sessions may be held as necessary. Every other year, the National Assembly elects someone to serve as president of the assembly. The National Assembly may draft laws, which are sent to the president, who has 15 days to approve or reject them.

This picture from a few days after the 2016 election shows the president (*front, left*), his cabinet, and the prime minister (*front, right*), before the office of prime minister was abolished.

Appointments to the Supreme Court are for life. The chief justice is chosen by the president. Chad also has a Constitutional Council, which is made up of nine judges elected to nine-year terms. This council reviews legislation, treaties, and all international agreements before they can officially be adopted.

The constitution of Chad allows for the recognition of local traditions and laws, so long as public order is maintained. Equality for all citizens and freedom of religion are also part of the constitutional guarantees.

In the 23 regions that make up Chad, many administrative posts are appointed by the president or the minister of the interior. These administrators do not have term limits. Instead, they remain in office until they are replaced. The person in charge of a region is called a governor. Before 2003, Chad was broken into 14 prefectures, and the prefects heading them retained their administrative duties after the switch. They work closely with the governors of each region, as well as with members of local assemblies. The people appointed to these assemblies are often tribal leaders or others who have a great deal of status in their communities.

In the 1960s, nine towns in Chad were granted municipal status by the government. They generated their own revenue through taxes, fines, and fees. The councils that run these towns are often directly elected by the townspeople. Those who are elected to the council vote among themselves to elect a mayor for the town. Many decisions made by these mayors and their councils, however, must be approved by the minister of the interior before they can be implemented.

HOW ELECTIONS WORK

Elections in Chad are different from how they are in the United States. Because most people in Chad cannot read, political parties write songs and have them played on the radio rather than having articles on their policies written up in newspapers. Trucks with loudspeakers will drive through villages and towns, playing the election songs for the various parties. One song for the MPS (the party of Idriss Déby) declares, "MPS, ma-nikhalu, ballat-na, ma yi-shallu," which roughly means, "MPS will not leave or abandon us, nor will they take our vote

On average, 62 percent of registered voters in Chad vote in presidential elections.

Idriss Déby was born in 1952. His father was a poor seminomadic herdsman of the Zaghawa ethnic group. Déby entered the military and was selected for pilot training, which he completed in 1976 in France. He was active in the military after returning to Chad and by 1982 had been promoted to commander in chief by Hissène Habré. In 1985, he was sent back to France for a senior officers' staff course and then returned home.

In 1989, Habré's regime turned on its Zaghawa supporters, killing many. Déby was accused of plotting to overthrow the government, and he and other Zaghawas in the military fled. Although Déby managed to reach Sudan and then Libya, others were captured and executed. With Libya's help, Déby formed and trained his own army.

In December 1990, he overthrew Habré's regime and became ruler of Chad. Almost immediately, Déby's regime proved to be just as brutal as the one it replaced— human rights advocates and civic leaders were intimidated, political opponents simply disappeared, and many people were arrested for opposing the regime.

Déby has been criticized for his corrupt government, but he has remained in office for 30 years.

away." People in the trucks will pass out T-shirts or other gifts to encourage people to vote for their candidate.

On election day, the trunks of trees are painted white as part of the national celebration. As most of the Chadian electorate is illiterate, voters are given pieces of paper, each one with a different candidate's picture on it. At the polls, the voters put their thumbprint on the paper that has the picture of the candidate they wish to vote for. The ink they use stains their finger and proves that they have voted. It also keeps anyone from voting twice.

Every Chadian citizen over the age of 18 has the right to vote as long as they have not been convicted of a felony, or serious crime.

POLITICAL UNREST

Chad still faces problems in turning itself into a democratic nation. The laws of the land are often ignored, especially by the military forces and some branches of the government.

Newspapers in Chad are often intimidated by the government. However, many see it as their duty to report the news truthfully, especially when it comes to politics.

Though the constitution of Chad grants its people civil rights, the majority of its prison population is made up of people who have been arrested and held without trial. People accused of being criminals have been tortured and sometimes executed without trial, and some units of the military are so out of control that they have been accused of killing shopkeepers for their money.

Unlike in the United States, prisoners in Chad are not fed; their families must provide their food. Sometimes the prisoners' visitors can walk up to the jail's windows to hand food over.

Complaints about the treatment of prisoners and other civil rights issues are taken to judges, but many of them have been intimidated by the military or other governmental departments that are committing the crimes. Judges who try to get away from such government interference are dismissed.

There is at least one voice speaking out against the lawlessness that continues to threaten Chad's democracy, and that is the press. The newspapers and journals of Chad are almost uniformly anti-Déby and publish articles critical of him. One journal, *N'Djamena Hebdo*, uses editorial cartoons to ridicule Déby. Although officially Déby claims that Chad has a free press, newspaper offices are sometimes ransacked by government employees, and there have been instances where editors of journals and newspapers critical of Déby have been fined and sued for defamation.

For the moment, *N'Djamena Hebdo* is still being printed. It has won international awards for its advocacy of press freedom in Chad and its struggle to keep the government accountable. It is widely read by those in Chad who are literate, and many of them are willing to voice their opinions about the government, at least among those they trust.

Chad's progress toward democracy since independence has been shaky. Though the government currently supports a multiparty system and presidential elections, some international organizations have voiced concerns over whether the elections in Chad are held fairly. Election laws have been instituted, but some branches of the government regularly ignore them. Although the situation remains unstable, some Chadians, such as journalists, are trying to cast a spotlight on the problems of the current regime.

Although many towns and villages have elected mayors, it is often the traditional leader—a chief or a sultan—to whom people turn for the resolution of their property or marital disputes.

INTERNET LINKS

www.cia.gov/library/publications/the-world-factbook/geos/cd.html
This web page from the CIA's *World Factbook* includes a detailed fact list about the government of Chad.

ndjamenahebdo.chez.com
This is the official website of *N'Djamena Hebdo*.

ECONOMY

Local Chadian economies are driven by open-air markets where people, such as these antique dealers, sell their wares.

WHEN CHAD WON ITS independence in the 1960s, its economy was mostly dependent on cotton. Other businesses were small and local, and industry and transportation were underdeveloped. Unfortunately, the country was soon hit with a drought that lasted throughout the 1960s and 1970s. This created a huge problem for the country: Farmers were unable to grow enough crops to sell—sometimes not even enough to feed themselves. Without agriculture, the economy was in desperate trouble, and Chad was forced to rely on international aid for its survival.

Several problems continue to keep Chad's economy depressed. It has no harbors, no railroads, and few paved roads. Transporting anything to a national market, let alone an international market, is an expensive, dangerous, and time-consuming undertaking. The only industry besides cotton is oil exportation, which has become increasingly important to the country and its position in international trade.

4

Chad's economy is expected to take a sharp downturn due to the global impact of the COVID-19 pandemic.

The currency of Chad is the Central African CFA franc.

OIL AND COTTON

In 2003, oil became Chad's main export, and today it makes up 60 percent of the country's national budget. The oil giant ExxonMobil operates as Esso in Chad. In 2019, the country produced around 140,000 barrels of oil per day, or 5.9 million gallons (22.3 million liters). Chad has four main oil production areas: the Doba Basin and the Doseo Basin in southern Chad; the Salamat Basin in eastern Chad; and the Lake Chad Basin near the border with Nigeria in western Chad.

Although it has brought money, employment, and international trade to the country, the oil industry in Chad is not without problems. Because Chad is landlocked, oil must travel through a pipeline to the Cameroonian port city of Kribi. The pipeline has been responsible for many oil spills and has impacted the health of both the people living near it and the environment. This, along with the misuse of the World Bank loan needed to build the pipeline, has brought criticism from international corruption watchdog groups and environmentalists.

Cotton is now Chad's second main export, although it employs more than 80 percent of the population. Chad ranks among the leading exporters of cotton around the world. Although cotton is native to the region, it was not until the French arrived and required cotton to be grown that it became an important cash crop.

Most of Chad's cotton is exported to Germany. The regions of Mayo-Kebbi Est and Ouest, Logone Oriental, and Moyen-Chari grow the most cotton and together produce almost half of the country's crop. Cotton is planted around mid-June and harvested in November.

Gum arabic is the resin of the acacia tree used by pharmaceutical and food industries. By 1970, Chad was the fifth largest producer in the world of gum arabic, but drought in the 1970s and 1980s disrupted production.

MINERALS

Chad's industries and economy have not developed sufficiently to exploit the natural resources found in the country. Natural resources such as bauxite (aluminum ore) in the south and uranium in the north have not been exploited.

Salt miners collect natron to be sold at local markets. Very little is sold internationally.

ELECTRICITY

Electricity is needed for cooking, for staying cool or warm, for light, for work, for recreational activities, and for transportation. In Chad, however, less than 9 percent of the population has access to electricity. The rest have to burn wood to keep themselves warm, to cook, and to have light after dark.

Chad has only one power station, which is near the capital city. Thus, almost all Chadians who have electricity live in N'Djamena. Because the country must import the fuel needed to run the power station, the station is very expensive to operate. Unfortunately, this means that although Chadians are very poor, they must pay some of the highest prices in the world for electricity.

Even in villages close to the capital city, homes are not connected to the power grid.

In the north, rebels and land mines have kept development away. In the south, industry has not yet developed to mine the bauxite, which is found in Koro near Moundou.

Other minerals have also been found in Chad, such as silver and titanium. Traditionally, the only mining industry in the country has been the mining of natron, a type of salt, in areas that have dried up around Lake Chad. It is used for medicinal purposes as an antibacterial solution, for the tanning of animal hides, and for making soap.

HIV/AIDS AND THE ECONOMY

In 2019, 68 percent of the people in the world with HIV/AIDS lived in sub-Saharan Africa, a region in which Chad is located. It is estimated that 770,000 people in sub-Saharan Africa died of AIDS in 2018 alone; 3,100 of those people were Chadians. Across sub-Saharan Africa, it is estimated that at least 9 percent of the people there have HIV/AIDS. So far, Chad has not been as severely affected as some other countries, with 1.3 percent of the people estimated to

AIDS has forced many Chadian children to take care of themselves.

have HIV, a virus spread through blood and other bodily fluids that causes a deadly disease known as AIDS. Still, Chad faces some of the problems facing other areas of sub-Saharan Africa when it comes to this disease.

The economic impact of this disease has been enormous. HIV/AIDS most often strikes people who are in the prime of their lives. These people are the ones the community depends on to be farmers, herders, office workers, teachers, translators, and soldiers. They are usually the ones who are of child-bearing age. When they die, many children become orphans.

Industries that are needed to help spur economic growth cannot find enough workers. People who may be educated enough to work in the civil service are dying just when they are finishing their educations. The disease also disproportionately affects young women, who are often the victims of sexual assault, and prevents them from achieving economic equality.

When people die of AIDS and leave their children behind, many of these children have nowhere to go. Relatives may take them in, but if the children have no living relatives, or if their relatives are too afraid of HIV to take them into their homes, the children live on the streets. They are forced to beg and steal to survive.

The presence of these homeless children in the villages and cities keeps people from wanting to start businesses or invest in these areas. These children often die very young from drug abuse, alcoholism, violence, or AIDS. So far, around 120,000 children have been orphaned by AIDS in Chad.

The medical costs of the disease continue to mount as well. As more people get sick, more doctors, nurses, and other medical personnel are needed to care for them. Most countries in Africa, including Chad, have limited amounts of money to spend on health care.

Already in some countries, the cost of treating HIV/AIDS has risen to 90 percent of the total national health budget. Every other disease and medical condition, from childhood diseases to broken bones to pregnancy, must be funded by the other 10 percent.

In recent years, however, new infections of HIV have begun to decrease. In 2018, only 6,500 people were newly infected with HIV, compared to 7,400 in 2010. International organizations such as UNAIDS and UNICEF have stepped in to bring antiretroviral medicine and HIV prevention measures to the area. More than 50 percent of people living with HIV in Chad are now receiving treatment. This number was meant to be increased to 90 percent by 2020, but the COVID-19 pandemic put enormous strain on global health initiatives.

Chad faces many challenges in growing its economy. Uncertainties in the oil market, the impact of COVID-19, and the large number of people with HIV/AIDS mean that Chad will have to struggle just as its neighbors do to achieve and maintain economic growth.

INTERNET LINKS

www.se4all-africa.org/seforall-in-africa/country-data/chad
This web page from Sustainable Energy for All gives an overview of Chad's energy access.

www.unaids.org/en/regionscountries/countries/chad
UNAIDS, the United Nations' HIV/AIDS group, presents factsheets and statistics about the epidemic in Chad.

www.unicef.org/chad/hivaids
This web page from UNICEF, a global child rights organization, details the challenges of and solutions to HIV/AIDS among children in Chad.

www.worldbank.org/en/country/chad/overview
The World Bank offers details about the economic development of Chad, as well as information about next steps in growing the economy.

ENVIRONMENT

Oil pipelines are threatening the health and safety of Chad's ecosystem.

5

BEING LANDLOCKED AND MOSTLY desert, Chad has very limited access to water. In the Sahara and the Sahel, the people, animals, and plants all compete for the limited sources of water and food the land has to offer. In the south, although water is more abundant and the rainy season is longer, the problems do not go away. A growing population means there are always more people who need clean water and food.

Many problems plague Chad and other nations that border the Sahara, including air and water pollution, soil erosion, and a loss of biodiversity, or the variety and number of plants and animals in a region. These issues add up to a process called desertification, or when once-usable land turns into desert. Unfortunately, Chad is too poor to address many of the environmental problems it faces.

SUSTAINABLE DEVELOPMENT IN SUB-SAHARAN AFRICA

The 51 countries located south of the Sahara, including Chad, constitute sub-Saharan Africa. Sub-Saharan Africa has one of the highest population growth rates in the world, at approximately 3.2 percent per year. In contrast, the United States had an estimated growth rate of 0.6 percent in 2018. By 2050, it is projected that sub-Saharan Africa will be populated by 2.2 billion people if the estimates are correct.

In 2015, the UN agreed upon 17 Sustainable Development Goals (SDGs), set to be achieved by 2030. These goals are meant to promote socioeconomic equality around the world, and many focus on the environment. So far, sub-Saharan Africa is on track to meet three of the seventeen goals: gender equality, climate action, and "life on land," which calls for sustainable forest management, preventing desertification, and halting biodiversity loss. However, a lack of clarity about how to keep countries accountable for meeting these goals, as well as confusion about whose responsibility it is to meet them, has led to slow, inefficient progress.

On a country-wide level, the UN Development Programme has put the Chad National Adaptation Plan into place. This project works to integrate climate change adaptation into Chad's policy making and national budget. This involves tracking climate trends and making sure both the government and the people are aware of how their actions affect their environment.

When people learn how and why their local environment is being damaged, they are often eager to help fix it but may not have the resources to do so. In the past, environmental organizations have educated people on how their soil is being depleted through overuse and how they can use different farming techniques to help the soil rather than destroy it. They have also taught people how to conserve water, such as by using the water from their bucket showers to water the plants near their house or by planting their gardens in partial shade.

One problem is that past projects that have been implemented to help people, such as the drilling of wells, have not been followed up on. After the government or an international organization has provided the resources and left them behind, they will inevitably deteriorate to the point where no one can use them anymore. Today, more groups are recognizing the importance of teaching the locals how to maintain and repair the equipment so that the funds invested in local development do not go to waste.

WHAT TO DO ABOUT WATER

In Chad, only 43 percent of the population has access to drinking water, and only 10 percent has access to sanitation services such as waste removal. Water sources are often polluted, and diarrheal diseases from polluted water remain the number one cause of death throughout the country. Getting clean water to the landlocked people of Chad has been a humanitarian crisis for many years.

Recently, organizations such as UNICEF have begun teaching young people how to build water filters, fix local wells and water pumps, make soap, and build latrines. Tackling both water insecurity and the lack of sanitation are key in improving Chad's water crisis. In the future, technology such as the Majik Water device, which harvests water from the air and works off-grid, may also play a large role in bringing safe water to billions of people across Africa.

Boys fill drums with water and cart them to the dry, remote parts of Chad.

In 2003, President Déby opened a spigot at this facility and connected Chad's pipeline to the Atlantic Ocean.

THE OIL PIPELINE

One of the greatest threats to Chad's environment is the Chad-Cameroon oil pipeline. Chad's biggest economic development has been the discovery of oil, but it must export its oil to other countries if it wishes to help its citizens climb out of poverty. However, this very thing also threatens its environment.

The pipeline project was started by oil companies in 2000, led by ExxonMobil. They formed a coalition to build a 665-mile (1,070 km) pipeline that would carry oil from Chad to Cameroon. The Chad-Cameroon pipeline was completed in 2003 and cost approximately $4.1 billion. To help the people of Chad, the oil companies and the government of Chad brought in the World Bank as an investor and guarantor. This means the World Bank could impose conditions on the oil companies and the Chadian government. It also provided more than $200 million for the construction of the pipeline.

To calm investors' fears that it would take the money without building the pipeline, the Chadian government requested that no money be transferred to the country until all the banking arrangements and conditions placed on the revenue had been approved and finalized. Until the money is disbursed, it is held in a bank account outside the country. According to the agreement, 10 percent of the oil revenue will be held in the account for future generations.

From the revenue the oil will generate, $19.3 billion was earmarked to be spent on road improvements. Two major roads, Bisney-Goura and Ngoura-Bokoro, were paved. Also, $4.9 billion was allocated to education. Most of the money was meant to build classrooms and buy books, desks, and other supplies for students.

People whose houses were in the way of the pipeline were offered $1,000 or compensation in the form of equipment, bicycles, sewing machines, and fruit trees. Because of the remoteness of some regions, cash is not always as helpful to people as such supplies. The total amount paid out to individuals was roughly $12 million for the affected areas in both Chad and Cameroon. Besides payment to individuals, payments were also made to communities to offset the economic losses they faced due to the construction of the pipeline.

Some villages were promised schools; others were promised wells, because nearly 60 percent of the population does not have access to safe drinking water. The World Bank offered to lend the money to Chad in exchange for promises that 80 percent of the money gained from oil revenues would be spent on infrastructure, public health, social welfare programs, and education; 5 percent on local development near the pipeline; and 10 percent to be held for future generations. The rest was meant to be used for general expenditures.

Chad received its first oil revenues in 2004 in the amount of $84.6 million. This increased Chad's national income by 31 percent in 2004 alone. Chad continued seeing double-digit growth in its income, entirely from revenue from its oil exports.

In 2005, Chad's government announced its plans to change its agreement with the World Bank by passing new legislation concerning the oil revenues. If passed, the fund for future generations would be scrapped and the oil revenue

Animals and plants become extinct for several reasons. They may be killed by people for food or destroyed because they are in the way of human development. Another reason could be that a new species is introduced to the region and it breeds faster or uses resources better than the species that were there before. This new species may have been brought by people.

A third way animals become extinct is through the side effects of human activity. When we cut down forests for timber and firewood or drain swamps to build houses, we destroy the homes of many animals. Some of them cannot survive anywhere else and will die off.

Animals in Chad, such as the elephant and the chimpanzee, are threatened because people are destroying the areas where they live and because the production and shipping of oil through the pipeline result in soil contamination.

The changing environment in Chad has threatened elephant populations, but whole herds can be seen in Zakouma National Park.

would not only be channeled to areas such as agriculture, education, and health care, but also to military spending.

The government also planned to change the law to allow it to spend up to 30 percent of the oil revenue. These actions angered officials at the World Bank as well as members of civil and human rights organizations in Chad. Some worried that the new laws and increase in military spending reflect instability from within Idriss Déby's government. This began a tense time between Chad and the World Bank, and in 2008, when the loan was paid off, the World Bank withdrew its support from the country.

Humans are not the only ones who suffer from the creation of the pipeline and the reallocation of oil revenues. Though the pipeline brings money to Chad, it also threatens wildlife such as chimpanzees, gorillas, and elephants. These animals live in the rain forest that the pipeline passes through. Chimpanzees and gorillas are endangered species. Scientists estimate that they will exist in the wild only for 10 to 50 more years if nothing changes. Some people estimate that the African elephant will be extinct in the wild within 20 years. In the end, while the pipeline may bring revenue to Chad, the consequences of its construction and continued presence may leave the country with more liabilities than benefits.

LOCUST CONTROL

Locust control is very important in the Sahel region, which includes large parts of Chad. Locusts are a kind of grasshopper that eat any plant they come across. Swarms of the insects often sweep across Africa, devouring everything they find, which leaves farmers, who are making a meager existence from the land, with nothing. Just one locust swarm can affect millions of people in many countries.

In 2004, seven African countries, including Chad, cooperated with the World Bank's International Development Association for the Africa Emergency Locust Project, in order to find ways to control the damage caused by locusts. Each country was responsible for its own strategy to limit and contain locust swarms and save crops. By 2005, all seven countries involved in the project had specific locust-control plans in place.

Farmers in Chad cannot afford to allow crops such as these salad greens to be destroyed by locusts.

One way to control locusts is by spraying pesticides on the swarms. The pesticides kill the locusts but also pollute the plants and the ground. Still, because it is an effective means of control, nearly 42,500 square miles (110,074 sq km) of land in Africa was sprayed in 2004.

Scientists continue to search for ways to control the unpredictable outbreaks of locusts so that subsistence farmers in Chad will not need to fear a loss of their livelihood every summer. However, even in 2020, swarms of locusts continued to threaten crops in Chad.

In the future, people might be able to control locusts by other means. For instance, people might use a fungus, *Metarhizium anisopliae*, that is deadly to locusts. It is thought to be harmless to plants, animals, people, and most other insects.

Scientists seek to control the locust swarms and do not want to eliminate them entirely. Locust swarms are part of the natural cycle of the region, and no one is sure what the side effects would be if they were eliminated entirely.

Chadians realize the importance of their natural environment to their survival. Unfortunately, many ecological problems have arisen as a result of economic development. As most Chadians still rely on the land for their livelihoods, problems such as these will not only threaten natural wildlife but also entire communities as well. Steps taken now can guarantee the future of the soil and the water, and thus secure the future of the people of Chad.

INTERNET LINKS

www.adaptation-undp.org/projects/chad-national-adaptation-plan
This web page outlines the UN Development Programme's Chad National Adaptation Plan.

sdgcafrica.org
The Sustainable Development Goals Center for Africa provides information about the SDGs and how they are being used to improve life in countries such as Chad.

CHADIANS

The people of Chad are not particularly patriotic, but their national flag remains an important symbol of the country's unity.

6

BECAUSE OF ITS HISTORY AS A crossroads through the middle of Africa, Chad is incredibly diverse. More than 200 ethnic groups can be found in Chad, each with their own culture and way of life. Although many live side by side in villages and cities, the cultural differences, conflict, and sometimes outright prejudice between these groups has made nation-building difficult. Most people's first allegiance is to their own group, not to their neighbors or the country at large.

Arabs are the third largest ethnic group in Chad but make up only around 9.7 percent of the population.

THE SARA PEOPLE

The largest ethnic group in Chad is the Sara. The Sara are sedentary farmers and fishermen living in the south of the country who are divided into clans. A few of the clans are the Ngambay, the Mbai, the Gulay, the Sar, and the Kaba, though there are many others.

The main social group among the Sara is the lineage, or family—called the *qir ka* among the eastern Sara, the *qin ka* among those living in the center of the region, and the *qel ka* among the western groups. Lineage

The life expectancy of Chadians is one of the lowest in the world, yet it is on the rise. In 1964, life expectancy was 29 years for men and 35 years for women. In 2020, it had risen to 56.5 years for men and 60.1 years for women.

Compared to the United States, this figure is still very low and reflects the lack of adequate health care and proper nutrition among Chadians. Although the government is trying to address these issues, Chad continues to face major problems in trying to ensure that all Chadians have access to health care, clean water, and adequate food supplies.

names refer to male ancestors. People identify with the lineage of their father, and rights to land are passed on from father to son.

The main social unit of the Sara is the extended family, which includes all married and unmarried brothers (and the married brothers' wives), their unmarried sisters, and their children. Family members may live in an enclosure together, with many such family units forming a village. Each family within the enclosure manages their affairs independently from other families in the village.

If all the people of a Sara village are from the same lineage, the village may be led by a single group of elders. If several lineages share a village, elders from the different groups will often come together to try to resolve problems between lineages. In such cases, the elders from the lineage that first moved into the area have senior status.

Very few Sara have converted to Islam. Catholic and Protestant missionaries have converted many, but some Sara still follow their native religion. Because of their proximity to the French-controlled districts of Chad, some Sara capitalized on the opportunity for education that could lead to positions in the armed forces and civil administration. Even today, many positions of authority within the government are still held by the Sara.

Noi is the name of a small Sara caste whose members function as priests. The Noi do not marry outside their caste, and their numbers are estimated to be fewer than 1,000. The installation of a Sara village chief requires the services of a Noi.

Water wells allow
desert nomads to
continue their way
of life.

THE ARABS

The Arabs of Chad are Muslim seminomadic herders of camels, horses, cattle, goats, and sheep. They spread out across northern Chad during the rainy season when food and water is most plentiful, but they live sedentary lives during the dry season to conserve resources. They are often found living among their sedentary neighbors as far south as N'Djamena.

The Arab family unit is called the *kashimbet*, which is led by an elder male called the *shaykh*. He, his wives, and his descendants make up the kashimbet. They live near each other and follow the same migration paths. Loyalty to one's kashimbet is considered very important.

Marriage is a community matter for Chadian Arabs. It is meant to reinforce kinship bonds, and it is common for first cousins to marry for this very reason.

The Haddad clan lives in the north of Chad. They speak the local language of wherever they are found and do not have their own common language. The Haddad keep to themselves, live on the fringes of others' villages, and rarely intermarry with other ethnic groups.

They are skilled workers who are often involved in iron working, weaving, dyeing cloth, tanning leather, and making shoes. Their neighbors often despise and fear them, however, because of the menial work they do and because they are said to practice magic.

The shaykhs from each family make the match, and when it comes time for the wedding, family and friends escort the bride to her husband's house in a celebratory parade.

Historically, Arabs have stayed out of Chad's affairs. Although their culture and religion have influenced the country immeasurably, the people themselves are indifferent to the state's existence. During the colonial period, the Arabs' refusal to recognize French authority allowed them to avoid the social and political changes that were affecting their neighbors. Today, a similar attitude toward the Chadian government keeps the Arabs free to do as they please.

THE TOUBOU PEOPLE

The Toubou live in the north of Chad. The two main branches of this ethnic group are the Teda and the Daza. Historically, they have been antagonistic toward each other and do not recognize each other as part of the same tribe.

The Toubou herd animals and cultivate crops at oases. Some mine for salt. Toubou families are formed by the parents and their children, and perhaps other relatives who need a place to stay. They travel with other families in bands, but membership of the bands changes from season to season.

Every Toubou belongs to a clan. Identifying with a clan is important as it establishes a person's place in Toubou society. Within a clan, everyone counts their descent from the same ancestors and shares the same cultural symbols and taboos.

Clans have recognized ownership over certain natural resources such as palm groves, springs, and pastures. Other clans may not use these resources without permission.

Conflicts between families only affect family honor, not the honor of the entire clan. If a Toubou is murdered, the victim's family will often seek revenge on either the killer or their relatives. Failing that, negotiations will secure the payment of a *goroga*, or blood price, which is often paid in camels. When men take more than one wife, the wives are usually from different clans and will have their own separate living quarters.

The Toubou people tend to be nomadic, but they are connected across the Sahara by their clans.

Because of the political unrest in Chad's neighboring countries, refugees often flee over the borders to find safety. There are more than 455,000 refugees in Chad. Around 300,000 are from Sudan, 70,000 are from the Central African Republic, and 8,000 are from Nigeria and other countries. Refugee camps have been set up in eastern Chad, and some people have been living there for at least 16 years.

The country's food and water shortages make taking care of refugees a difficult task. Although Chad receives help from the UN, housing, feeding, and educating hundreds of thousands of people is considered a humanitarian crisis when there are barely enough resources to sustain the citizens of the country.

Nigerians who have fled the violence in their home country gather to pray in a UN refugee camp in Chad.

THE FULANI PEOPLE

The Fulani are nomadic and seminomadic herders who have converted to Islam. They refer to themselves as Fulbe and call their language Fulfulde. They first settled in what is now Chad in the 15th century. After their conversion to Islam, their settlement at Chekna became a center for religious studies for Fulani from all over Central and West Africa.

The Fulani raise cattle and farm millet and corn. A family needs about 100 cattle to be self-sufficient. The corn, which ripens more quickly than the millet, provides food while the Fulani wait for the millet to ripen. Millet and milk are the most important parts of the Fulani diet.

The Fulani do not live in settled villages but often roam with their cattle during the rainy season. During the dry season, cattle are concentrated around the few remaining watering holes and are kept on the fields where, during the

Fulani women are responsible for building their homes and taking good care of their children.

rainy season, the Fulani grow their millet. Thus the cattle manure fertilizes the fields during the dry seasons.

If the rainy season is a bad one, however, there might not be enough rain to saturate the soil, and the large quantities of cattle manure on the fields often lead to fires, making the land unusable for several seasons. Men tend the cattle, while the women are usually less nomadic, building houses in small clusters near watering holes.

A woman will collect the materials to build her house herself, but her friends, family, and children may also help. The house is considered to belong to the woman, as are the responsibilities for household duties such as raising the children and cooking.

The overriding bond in Fulani society is between mother and child, not between man and woman as it is in the West. A Fulani man looking for a wife will seek someone who will be a good mother to his children. For the first few years of life, a young child will always be within arm's reach of their mother.

A child will be with their mother while she works at home or will be carried on her back if she needs to go out. A baby who cries is immediately picked up and nursed. A Fulani woman who lets her baby cry is considered a bad mother.

Though the Fulani are Muslims, they do not speak Arabic, and few send their sons to Koranic (or Quranic) schools. Those who are educated in Koranic schools are well respected, but people often would rather ask a village elder for advice.

Many Fulani carry charms and believe in magic. Most know how to prepare love potions. Men are said to use them to get women to love them, while women use them to keep their husband's eyes from wandering. Most women do not want their husband to take more wives, even though this is customary.

The Fulani see marriage as a gradual process rather than something attained in a single ceremony. During the betrothal, the bride will be taken to her future husband's mother's house where, on several occasions, she will run back to her father's house. This process goes on for some time until the two are living together on a regular basis, but the marriage is still not considered complete until the first son is born.

Like other Muslims, the Fulani pray five times a day, but they do not necessarily pray at the same times of the day as other Muslim groups.

The government of Chad has had a difficult time getting people from different ethnic groups to come together as a unified nation. The multitude of ethnic groups and languages has been a barrier to creating a peaceful Chad. As Chad emerges more prominently on the international stage, however, the people of the country will have good reason to work together harmoniously for a brighter future.

INTERNET LINKS

chadembassy.us/index.php/the-country/population-society
This web page from the Chadian embassy discusses the diverse population of the country.

www.cia.gov/library/publications/the-world-factbook/geos/cd.html
The CIA's *World Factbook* includes a section about the people and society of Chad.

LIFESTYLE

In N'Djamena, street markets sell local
food and handmade items.

LIFE IS VERY DIFFERENT IN THE RURAL and urban parts of Chad. In rural areas, which make up most of the country, very few people have access to electricity. Even fewer have cars. Houses are mud or straw huts arranged into small villages, and food is cooked over fire. The people grow crops or herd animals to feed their families. Many people are nomadic and move across the country regularly to find feeding grounds for their livestock.

In urban areas, and particularly in N'Djamena, people own luxuries such as cars, radios, and televisions. They ride bicycles, dine at restaurants, and go to the movies. Most city dwellers work in the farming industry, but others work for the government, for banks, or for private businesses. Many people live in apartments like people in most cities around the world.

Across Chad, communities are run by men, and they are often the sole breadwinners of their families. They take on leadership roles, and most teachers, doctors, and nurses are male.

WOMEN'S ROLES

In Chad, women have very different lives from most women in the United States. They are expected to have large families, and girls have very little access to education or modern conveniences.

7

The average family in Chad has six or seven children.

Women often get up very early to perform household chores such as sweeping their courtyard. Later in the morning, they go to the market to exchange surplus goods or produce for the items they need for their home. Afternoons are often filled with work such as grinding grain or shelling peanuts. Women will often sing and joke with one another as they perform these routine tasks to make it more enjoyable.

Women are often the ones who work the land. They plant and tend the sesame, peanut, and millet crops. If there are loads to carry, women will carry them on their heads, even if they are very heavy. They must also gather wood, make fires, and cook for their families.

Many Chadian women are widows, their husbands having died due to war or disease. That leaves them to do the household work and also somehow earn enough money to make up for whatever wages their husbands would have brought home. Sometimes women have other family members who can help them, but their lives are still very hard.

Girls in Chad are expected to grow up quickly to take care of their families.

Women usually have many children. Unless a woman is very lucky, at least one of her children will die due to some childhood disease or accident. The older children will often have to help around the house and also take care of their younger siblings, allowing their mother to get more work done.

CHILDREN

Children living in the capital city are more likely than others to go to school. Even so, they can also be found helping their families by selling vegetables and fruits in the markets. They may also help their mothers look after younger siblings, cook the meals, and clean the house.

Children must walk to and from school, as there is no public transportation to get them there. The school is likely to be in a one- or two-room building with walls made of clay and a roof of tin. The teachers will teach students from multiple grades at the same time. While the teacher is working with one age group, the others will be busy with their own assignments.

The teacher rarely gives the children homework, as most children will be busy at home helping their parents. There is always so much to do around the house that the children are needed to help out whenever they can. During the rainy season, when the seeds must be sown, the children will not go to school so that they can help their parents in the fields. Having many children is expensive but it also means the parents have more hands to help in the fields, with herding the animals, or in the family business. Fathers will teach their sons how to help in their offices or shops.

Children have time for play, but they learn about their responsibilities to their families at a young age. Whether it is gathering firewood, drawing water

Chadian children find ways to play even when life can be hard.

from a well, sweeping the house, or babysitting a younger brother or sister, every child has a role to play in a Chadian family.

There are school breaks during the planting and harvesting seasons so that the children can help their family in the fields. Even young children are sent out into the fields for days at a time to line strings along each row of the crop. The strings are decorated with strips of bags, wire, or other shiny things. The child sits in the shade and waits for the birds to come and try to feed on the crops. When the birds come, the child pulls the string, and the birds fly away, startled by the flapping things on the string.

FAMILY MATTERS

Chadians are very concerned with family. Adult children often live near their parents, and elderly people usually live with or near one of their sons. Polygamy is very common, even in Christian areas. Children of the same mother and father are usually very close, and they are also likely to be close to their half-sisters and half-brothers. All children by the same father are considered brothers and sisters, even if they have different mothers. People use the term "cousin" when referring to members of their extended family.

Extended family members are important when people wish to find jobs or a place to live in a new town. People will often call upon their distant relatives when such help is needed.

In the family, men make the important decisions while women are in charge of the house and domestic responsibilities. They raise the children, cook, and sew. Women in the south have more freedom to travel and are more likely to have their own money compared to women in the north, where Muslim families often keep their daughters and wives inside family compounds, which they cannot leave without permission. Southern women may earn money by selling milk, yogurt, and spices in the market.

Young people rarely date, as many marriages are arranged by their families. Girls are expected to help their mothers as soon as they are able, and they are unlikely to have much free time as they have to take care of their younger siblings too. By the time they are teenagers, girls are expected to marry.

Men may wait until their 20s to find a wife because many ethnic groups in Chad require the young man to give a gift to the bride's parents before he can marry their daughter. It may take the young man some time to accumulate this, so he will most likely be somewhat older than his bride. During the time the young man is preparing for marriage, he will get to know the woman's father and brothers; once he has done that, he will be able to spend some time with his intended bride.

Local celebrations, such as weddings, can be time-consuming but festive affairs; however, some weddings can consist of a simple payment of a bride price to be considered complete. Among some groups in Chad, a couple is only considered married once the woman becomes pregnant or gives birth to a son.

GETTING MARRIED

In the south, women in the village usually take a week to make preparations for a Christian wedding. They sit on straw mats in small groups and chat while they sift flour, grind wheat and millet, and fry dough into something similar to doughnuts. Goats and chickens are killed and their meat prepared. Meanwhile, children run around squealing and getting underfoot, and the women sing songs and clap their hands. The atmosphere is very joyous.

During this week of preparation, one night is set aside for people to form a line and present gifts to the bride and the groom. The gift might be a goat or a sheep. Other common presents are household items such as pots, pans, other cooking utensils, bowls, and soap. After the gift-giving, the men perform traditional dances wearing animal furs and sing celebratory songs.

Mothers in N'Djamena bring their children with them to sell items at the local market.

On the day of the wedding, the bride and the groom ride in a car while the entire village walks behind. Everyone goes to the church for the ceremony. Some people will stick their heads in the windows so they can see what is going on. A few elements of the wedding ceremony have been borrowed from the West: The bride often wears a white dress, and the couple kisses at the end of the ceremony.

Muslim ceremonies last for days and include a great deal of feasting and gift-giving. Islamic law allows a man to have up to four wives at once, but he must treat them all equally. New wives are often seen as rivals by the first wife and will not be welcomed, though sometimes co-wives manage to get along well.

Muslim weddings are considered to be a contract between two people made in the presence of Muslim witnesses and the bride's father or guardian. The groom is required to give the bride a gift. The gift can be cash or something else, such as herd animals if that is what the groom possesses. The gift will be specified in the marriage agreement, though the actual payment can be put off until a later date.

The bride may or may not be present when the contract is made. If she is not present, her father or guardian must ask her in the presence of two witnesses if he has her permission to make the contract with the groom and if she agrees to the gift that has been proposed.

THE EDUCATION SYSTEM

Formal, structured educational programs were not introduced to Chad until 1920, two decades after it came under French control. Such programs began small and progressed slowly. By 1933, Chad had only 18 trained teachers. The largest school had only 3 grades and 135 enrolled students.

By the 1950s, enrollment had climbed to more than 17,000 students, the bulk of whom were in public schools. In Christian areas, private schools had been established by missionaries, but no such private schools were available in the Muslim areas of the country. This was due to Muslim resistance to sending their children to Western-style schools and because boys were already

being educated in Arabic at small Koranic schools, which provided religious instruction and some general education. For many people, this was sufficient education. Also, lessons in public schools were taught in French, which was not spoken by many people. Students entered school only to be confronted by a language they did not speak at home.

Most of the students sent to school by their parents were boys. Parents usually did not consider a girl's education necessary, since girls could only look forward to a life of marriage, child care, and taking care of the family's home. Boys, however, were not much better off. At best, schools offered only a few years of instruction. Literacy rates remained very low.

By the time Chad became independent in 1960, there were only three secondary schools in the entire country. Student enrollment in Chad was only

Even today, many young girls in Chad do not get the opportunity to go to school because they are responsible for helping their families.

about 11 percent. Anyone who wanted to get a higher education had to have the means to leave the country. Since most people make their living through subsistence farming, they could not afford to get more than the bare minimum of an education for their children.

Chad took a big step in the early 1970s with the founding of the University of N'Djamena. Due to the outbreak of hostilities in the late 1970s, however, the university was closed in 1978. The campus was looted during the 1979 and 1980 battles in the capital. Teachers went back to their home villages and returned to farming while the civil wars raged.

The university reopened in 1984 and had 1,500 students by 1988. However, because schools had not been staffed by trained professionals and the students' education had been interrupted by years of violence and uncertainty, students were unprepared for academic studies. In 1994, 86 percent of secondary students failed their university entrance exams.

Today, the situation has improved, and the university has seven schools: the School of Education, the School of Humanities and Social Sciences, the School of Legal and Political Sciences, the School of Languages and Communication Arts, the School of Exact and Applied Sciences, the School of Human Health, and the School of Economics and Management. Degree programs include sociology, geography, history, law, economics, modern literature, French, English, Arabic, mathematics, and physics, as well as biology, chemistry, and geology. The university also offers two doctorate programs, one in science and one in humanities.

Primary education in Chad consists of a six-year program. Once completed, the student earns a primary school certificate. In the south, students often start school at age 6; in the north, they are often older. Subjects include reading, writing, spelling, grammar, mathematics, history, geography, science, and art.

Secondary education in Chad follows the French model. Students who have their primary certificate compete to get into two types of schools: the college or the lycée. The college offers a four-year course, the lycée a seven-year course. At the end of these terms, the students take exams that are a requirement for entry to the university.

HEALTH CONCERNS

Most people in Chad do not have access to modern health care. One of the diseases facing Chadians is malaria, which is spread by mosquitoes. It is caused by a parasite passed from mosquito to human through bites. The parasite enters the body through bloodstream and travels to the liver, where it can lie dormant for up to a year before maturing and infecting red blood cells. Symptoms include headache, fever, chills, muscle aches, and vomiting. The disease can result in brain swelling, breathing problems, organ failure, coma, or death. Although there are antimalarial drugs that will kill the parasite or

Health centers such as this one work with local communities to make sure children are vaccinated.

TRADITIONAL MEDICINE

Traditional medicine is the indigenous medical knowledge of a culture, generally dating back to before colonization and the introduction of Western, modern medicine. Traditional healers use plants and natural practices to deal with illnesses, pregnancies, and sometimes even spiritual afflictions attributed to witchcraft.

In Central Africa, including Chad, there continues to be a heavy reliance on traditional medicine stemming from distrust in modern medicine. Between the 1920s and 1950s, French campaigns to slow the spread of a disease called sleeping sickness forced many in the area to take medications that caused blindness and death. This made people suspicious and fearful of modern medicine.

Today, health organizations hope to work with traditional healers to earn the trust of Central African countries. Although traditional medicine is helpful in many situations, vaccines and birth control are vital modern tools that are necessary for the health and growth of countries such as Chad.

prevent someone from being infected, there is no commonly accepted and approved vaccine or other long-term solution.

Additionally, childhood diseases such as whooping cough, measles, and polio that are routinely prevented in wealthier areas of the world are a major problem in Chad. With enough vaccinations, these diseases could be controlled, if not eliminated entirely. Unfortunately, in some areas of Africa, including Chad, many people have boycotted the polio vaccine. Polio is a disease that affects the nervous system and is carried via contaminated water. It causes paralysis, atrophied muscles, and sometimes death. Although anyone can contract polio, young children are the ones most often affected.

Amid rising Muslim-Western tensions in 2004, Nigeria's Muslims led an immunization boycott. This boycott triggered an outbreak all across the continent, infecting children in neighboring countries including Benin, Chad, and Cameroon. Despite this and other outbreaks of vaccine-preventable illnesses, health organizations continue to see this attitude toward vaccines today.

Each year in Chad, many children die from disease or hunger before they reach the age of five. Getting health care to the people is difficult without the necessary infrastructure. Chad's remoteness means that health care must be delivered by truck or small airplane, and many people simply do not have access to those few places where health care is dispensed. Approximately 30 percent of Chad's population had access to health care in 1990. Today, that number is only slightly higher.

INTERNET LINKS

www.unicef.org/chad/education
This UNICEF web page details the education challenges in Chad, as well as the organization's proposed solutions.

www.who.int/workforcealliance/countries/tcd/en
This web page from the World Health Organization provides an overview of the goals of the Human Resources for Health (HRH) program in Chad.

RELIGION

Criers call Chadian Muslims to prayer five times a day from the tops of towers called minarets.

8

More than 52 percent of Chadians practice Islam, making it the most common religion in the country.

CHAD'S CONSTITUTION GUARANTEES freedom of religion, meaning that people are allowed to follow whatever religion they like. Many Chadians practice both a native religion and an imported religion such as Islam or Christianity. The native religions sometimes feature a creator god who made the universe and then retired from intervening in its affairs. This is why people appeal to spirits, who play active roles in this world, rather than to a god.

Because the belief in a creator god is already part of native traditions, people often find Christianity or Islam easy to embrace. They do not see a problem with believing in the Christian and Muslim God and yet turning to the ancestors and the spirits for guidance or assistance. For instance, a Muslim may pray to Allah (God) but wear a charm or drink ink that was used to write verses of the Quran to ward off disease or evil spirits.

Although members of these religions generally tolerate each other in Chad, conflict still exists. Within the government, the Muslim majority often tries to prioritize Muslim interests while the Christian minority pushes back. Chad continues to try to balance these differing viewpoints, and in many ways it has been successful. Chadian Muslims and Christians can even be found attending each other's celebrations and ceremonies.

NATIVE TRADITIONS

Many people in Chad continue to follow native traditions in one form or another. Practitioners of these native religions view the world as a complicated system of relationships among people (both living and dead), animals, plants, the forces of nature, and supernatural powers. All things are considered to have some sort of life force. The relationships among all these life forces are well-ordered and hierarchical, so that each has its own recognized and established place in the universe.

According to these religions, human societies reflect this hierarchy. For instance, people live with families, families live in villages, and villages are

MAGIC AND WITCHCRAFT

Whatever their religion, most Chadians believe in magic and witchcraft. Some people act as magicians to help others determine the will of the spirits. Most Chadians would not hesitate to consult such people. Magicians are said to use magic, which can be bad or good, to help or harm. Everyone knows who the magicians are; they can be asked to help someone get his or her health back or to bring good luck. Sorcerers, however, work in secret because their magic is always evil and they use it to siphon away and consume the energy of others.

When people suspect a sorcerer is nearby because bad luck or disease has struck a village, they will consult a magician to identify the sorcerer and find a way to stop the disruption of the natural order. A sorcerer, once revealed, will be punished, and rituals will be performed to appease the spirits and return the universe to balance.

headed by chiefs or a council of elders. Everyone has a place and lives by rules and laws that allow everyone to get along. People who break the rules or commit crimes act against this natural order. Their deeds invite bad luck because the order, once upset, will remain upset until it is rebalanced. If people act in an antisocial manner by disobeying the rules of their society, they invite chaos to attack the village—perhaps the crops will fail or the animals will sicken and die. Ritual acts such as prayers, sacrifices, and dances can restore the balance to the natural order. Restoring order protects the people, as well as their families, animals, and crops.

Ancestors are a very important part of this balance. They are seen as being able to intervene directly in human affairs because they bridge the gap between the natural world, having once been alive, and the supernatural world, being dead. The ancestors most prone to intervene are those who have recently died, since it is believed that it may take weeks or months for the newly departed spirit to fully cross over into the land of the dead. Many rituals are designed to appease these new spirits.

People follow certain practices to help them avoid the attention of bad spirits. They do not allow a child to sleep alone inside a house because an evil spirit may steal the child away. They will not compliment a child on their looks

Native African traditions are animistic. Animism is the belief that all people, animals, plants, and objects have souls or spirits.

for fear of making a bad spirit jealous. Also, people will not whistle after dark, because it could attract the attention of wicked spirits.

The Sara celebrate the harvest by going through the newly harvested fields with nets and fire, trying to catch the ancestors. The ancestors are then offered plenty to drink, while the living eat the first meal made with the new crop.

FOLLOWING ISLAM

Islam was founded by the Prophet Muhammad in the seventh century. Islam requires its followers to submit to Allah, which can be shown by following the five pillars of the faith. The five pillars are the performing of daily prayers; the giving of alms; fasting during Ramadan; participating in the *hajj*, or pilgrimage, to Mecca; and proclaiming that there is no god but Allah and that Muhammad is his prophet. The word of God as revealed to Muhammad is found in the Muslim holy book, the Quran. The sayings of Muhammad are collected in the hadith.

Although Muslims can worship anywhere, many go to traditional mosques such as this one in Faya.

People in Chad observe the five pillars a little differently than other Muslims do. For example, public prayers may take place more often than the usual once a week, and they rarely, if ever, take place inside a mosque.

During the centuries since its founding, different sects have arisen within Islam. One of them is Sufism, which is differentiated from other forms of Islam by its insistence on achieving direct personal experience with the divine. Some Muslims believe that Sufis are not really Muslims at all, but Sufis believe that they are practicing a pure form of the religion by adhering to its original traditions. A Sufi seeks the truth, which they believe can be found only within oneself. Sufis are divided up into brotherhoods, or orders, that attempt to spread Islam throughout the world. Some of these brotherhoods can be found in Chad.

The Grand Mosque of N'Djamena attracts Muslims from all over the city.

One Sufi order in Chad is the Sennusiya. The brotherhood originated in northern Libya in the 19th century. Their members advocate a return to the fundamental principles of Islam and avoidance of foreign influences. Unlike other orders, the Sennusiya reject music, dancing, singing, and all forms of luxury.

In the mid-20th century, another order, the Tidjaniyya, became predominant in Chad. This order was favored by the French throughout their tenure due to the religion's focus on submission to earthly authorities. It was fully established in Chad by the 1950s. However, a new wave of Islamic fundamentalism from Sudan has weakened the influence of the Tidjaniyya in Chad today.

One reason Islam may have had better luck in attracting African converts than Christianity was that Islam was associated with the successful traders who came across the Sahara, while Christianity was associated with the hated colonial government. The traders looked like the Chadians, dressed like them, spoke their languages, and also shared a similar culture. Thus, Chadians were more receptive to the Islamic religion. Christian missionaries did not have the same advantage.

Although recently an influx in fundamentalist Islamic teachings has found some followers in Chad, so far their numbers are small. The calls for French to be removed as a national language and for all governmental proceedings to be held in Arabic have gone mostly unheeded.

FOLLOWING CHRISTIANITY

Christianity arrived in Chad in the early 20th century. Protestants arrived around the early 1920s, and the first Catholic missionaries arrived in 1929. However, organized efforts to convert the Chadians to Catholicism did not begin until 1946.

The Protestantism first brought to Chad was a fundamentalist version of Christianity from the United States. These missionaries frowned upon dancing, alcohol, and local superstitions. Early converts found it difficult to remain in their native villages because they were not able to take part in many aspects of village life, such as harvest rituals and communal prayers. Thus, the early

Protestants often had few converts, as the strictness of their religion did not win people over. Few were willing to give up their families and home villages for this foreign religion.

As more missionaries arrived, however, they set up schools and hospitals. They taught French, which enabled people to find work in the civil service of the colonial administration. These factors encouraged people to convert, and by the 1940s and 1950s, more people were attracted to Christianity. By 1980, Chad had approximately 80,000 Christian converts. These were mainly from the south, as the missionaries did not go to the heavily Muslim occupied areas of the north.

The late arrival of Catholic missionaries to Chad came as a result of politics. In the early 18th century, the Vatican (the center and ruling force of the Catholic faith) had declared that Catholicism would be brought to Chad by Italian missionaries, but it was the French, not the Italians, who were in control of Chad. It was only after World War II ended in 1945 that the French Roman Catholic missionaries came to Chad.

The Cathedral of Our Lady of Peace in N'Djamena is one of many Catholic churches in Chad.

Like Protestants, Catholics encouraged education and provided social services. In the 1980s, it was estimated that around 20,000 Chadians attended Roman Catholic schools. Many nuns who were sent to Chad were trained nurses who served in hospitals and clinics. This helped some people accept and convert to Catholicism.

Today, most people who are Christian in Chad practice a blend of their native traditions with the imported traditions of the Christian faith.

CEREMONIE D'INVESTITURE DU PRESIDENT DE LA REPUBLIQUE
حفل تنصيب رئيس الجمهورية
08 Aout 2016

Oaths of office in Chad, such as the presidential inauguration oath, exclude religions other than Islam even though half of the population follows a different faith.

RELIGIOUS CONFLICT

Most of the time, the various religions of Chad exist side by side with few problems, but sometimes tensions are high. The Islamist terrorist group Boko Haram has spread into Chad in recent years, and their frequent bombings have killed hundreds and displaced more than 100,000 people from their homes. Although the government has banned their extremist version of Islam, known as Wahhabism, upholding the ban has proved difficult. Religious leaders work to raise awareness of terrorist attacks and advocate for security around places of worship.

Religious conflict also takes place within the government. Even though the constitution separates religion and the state, the oath of office requires people to swear in the name of Allah, who not everyone swearing the oath believes in (or who some call by a different name). Some refuse to take the oath and are fired for it, giving the government a Muslim slant and discouraging people of other faiths from running for office in the first place. Christians advocate for the wording to be changed to simply "God," or for removing the religious element from the oath altogether to promote the neutrality called for by the constitution.

While a few people who have converted to Christianity from Islam have been shunned or even beaten by their families, the government itself does not force anyone to convert to any religion, nor have any incidents been reported in which terrorist organizations targeted religious establishments in the country. Other religious groups such as followers of Baha'i and Jehovah's Witnesses have been allowed into Chad, though they have not yet found many converts. Religious teachings are forbidden in public schools, but religious organizations are welcome to open schools of their own.

INTERNET LINKS

www.pbs.org/wgbh/pages/frontline/shows/saudi/analyses/wahhabism.html
These interviews from *PBS Frontline* discuss the threat of Wahhabism and its origins in Saudi Arabia.

www.state.gov/reports/2018-report-on-international-religious-freedom/chad/
This latest report from the U.S. Department of State details the status of religious freedom in Chad.

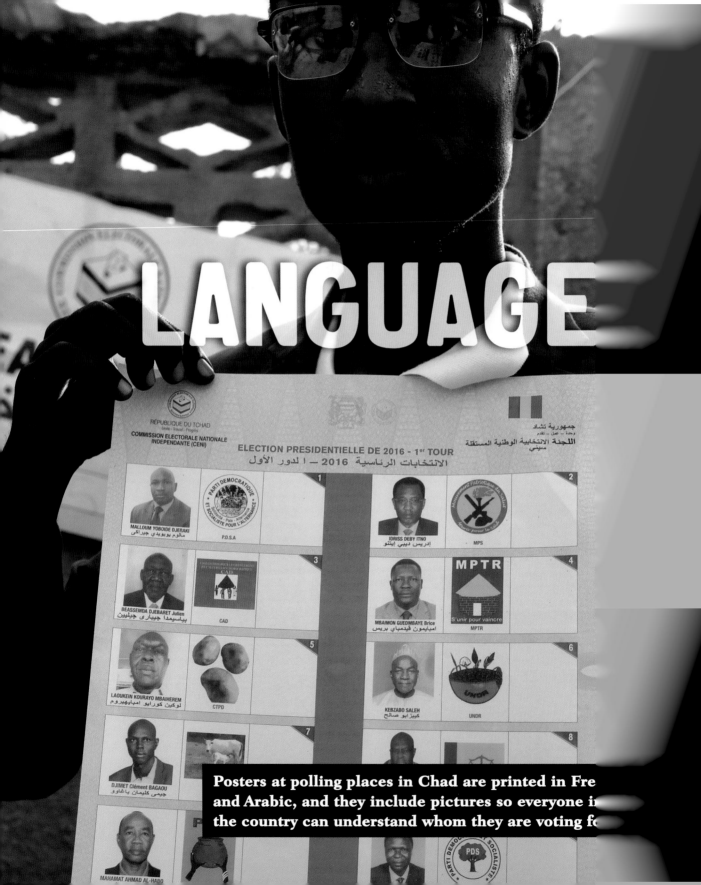

LANGUAGE

Posters at polling places in Chad are printed in Fre
and Arabic, and they include pictures so everyone i
the country can understand whom they are voting fo

9

FRENCH AND ARABIC ARE THE official languages of Chad. National communication and education are done in French, and when people from different parts of the country meet, they generally speak to each other in either language.

However, more than 120 languages and dialects are spoken throughout Chad. Many people in Chad are not fluent in either Arabic or French, but they may speak three or four of the native languages found in their immediate area. Many of these languages have never been extensively studied or are little known to the outside world. Some are spoken only by a few people of one ethnic group. Others, like the Sara language in the south, are spoken by large numbers of people.

This diversity of languages speaks to Chad's position as a crossroads. Throughout history, people passing through occasionally settled in the area, bringing their languages with them.

SPEAKING ARABIC

Arabic is spoken by more than 420 million people in the world today and is the official language for 25 countries. It is written from right to left and has 28 letters. Some of these letters have four forms—the forms they take at the beginning, the middle, or the end of a word, and the form they take when appearing alone. This can be confusing for people used to the Roman alphabet.

At least 50 languages in Chad are considered endangered, meaning that so few people speak them that they are on the brink of being forgotten.

The Arabic alphabet today has very ancient roots. It was developed from an Aramaic script used more than 2,000 years ago. However, Arabic has more sounds in it than Aramaic, so people could not use the alphabet as it was. Over the centuries, speakers of Arabic languages adapted the original alphabet into something that was more useful to them. The current form of the alphabet was developed around the seventh century.

Arabic is usually written without vowels or marks to indicate pronunciation (diacritical marks). However, the Quran is written with both because it is considered the word of Allah, and Muslims believe proper pronunciation of the word of Allah is vital.

Arabic is a Semitic language. Few Semitic languages are still in use. Of those few, Arabic is by far the most widespread and widely spoken. Others, such as Hebrew, which is spoken in Israel, and Amharic, which is the official language of Ethiopia, are some of the few Semitic languages that are still in use. Arabic is so widespread because it is the liturgical language of Islam. All Muslims are supposed to be able to read the Quran in its original language, which is classical Arabic. Many of these people, when they converted to Islam, learned Arabic for their everyday use as well.

Children sent to Muslim schools are taught classical Arabic and its script. Because the spoken Arabic of their area can be very different from the classical Arabic they learn in school, students are not necessarily able to read and write either modern standard Arabic or their local Arabic dialect upon graduation. They will know only classical Arabic.

More than 30 dialects of Arabic are used in Chad. They are spoken mostly in the north. Arabic was introduced with Islam in the 14th century. The Arabs of Chad divide themselves into three groups: the Juhayna, the Hassuna, and the Awlad Sulayman. The Juhayna arrived in the 14th century. The Hassuna came after them, and the Awlad Sulayman did not migrate to Chad until the 19th century. The Hassuna and the Awlad Sulayman, most of whom were herders or farmers, migrated from the area that is today Libya.

Because many Arabs earned their living as merchants, Chadic Arabic (also called Turku) became a trade language across the country. Until the 1970s,

Yes . . . . Na'am
No . . . . La
Thank you . . . . . Shukran
Good morning . . . Sabah al-Kheir

Some words and phrases in Arabic change depending on whether one is speaking to a man or a woman. For instance:

Please. . . . . Min fadlak *(to a man)*
. . . . Min fadlik *(to a woman)*
Pardon me . . . . . Samehni *(to a man)*
. . . . Samehini *(to a woman)*
How are you? . . . Kif halak? *(to a man)*
. . . . Kif halek? *(to a woman)*

much of the business in non-Arab towns, such as Sarh and Moundou, was conducted in Arabic. After the sectarian violence in the late 1970s, this practice was discontinued in some areas.

Arabic is also spoken among groups who are not Arab by ethnicity. Some of them were probably former slaves of Arab masters, such as the Yalna and the Bandala, but others have adopted the language after long exposure to Arabic-speaking neighbors.

One characteristic of Arabic is that it has what are called "sun letters" (*shams*) and "moon letters" (*qamar*). The Arabic word for "the" is often written in English as *al*. When a noun begins with a moon letter, the definitive article remains *al*, as in *al-qamar*, "the moon." When a noun begins with a sun letter, the word *al* changes its *l* for the initial consonant in the noun, thus, the sun is known as *ash-shams*.

Another feature of Arabic is its three-consonant roots. Any word that has the same three consonants in the same order will be about the same thing. Thus, any word with "k-t-b" will be about writing: *kitab* means "book," *kitub* means "writers," *maktub* means "letter," and *maktabheh* means "library."

At public schools in Chad, children are educated in French, making them more likely to speak the lauguage as they grow up.

SPEAKING FRENCH

More than 220 million people in the world speak French as their primary language. Another 72 million people speak it as a secondary language. This makes French the sixth most spoken language on the planet.

"Francophone" describes countries where French is spoken as the first or second language by the majority of the population. Chad, therefore, is part of what is called Francophone Africa, since French is one of its main languages.

French was introduced into the area in the late 19th century. When the French gained control of the area, it became the official language of government and of institution. At that time, Chad was part of what was called French Equatorial Africa.

Do you speak English? . . . . . . Parlez-vous anglais?

Excuse me . . . . Excusez-moi

Glad to meet you . . . . Enchanté

Good-bye. . . . . Au revoir

Good evening . . . . Bonsoir

Good day. . . . . Bonjour

How are you? . . . . Comment allez-vous?

I don't understand. . . . . Je ne comprends pas

I'm sorry . . . . Désolé

Please. . . . . S'il vous plaît

Thank you . . . . Merci

You're welcome . . . . De rien

French remains a very important second language for many people in Chad. Government documents and websites are generally in French. About 1,000 French expatriates live in Chad.

SPEAKING SARA

Many people in Chad speak some dialect of the Sara-Bagirmi language group. Sara dialects are spoken in the region between the towns of Moundou and Sarh. Sara is a tonal language and has three tones: ascending, flat, and descending. Tonal languages are very hard to learn because the same sounds spoken with different tones will mean different things.

In Sara, *mang* said with a flat tone means "ox" but pronounced with a descending tone, it means "buy," and when said in an ascending tone, it means "cigarette." Someone whose first language is English, French, or Arabic may not be able to discern the differences, and this can be confusing for them.

Sara has words for only three colors—black, white, and red. Every other color is described by using the word *nyere* ("color") and then an object of that

French is the trade language in Chad. Haggling in street markets, such as this one in Faya, is often done in French between people who do not understand each other's native languages.

color. A yellow bowl could be called "a bowl the color of the sun," or a green shirt might be "a shirt the color of a leaf."

Some people use French words for colors that have no name in Sara. Also, there is no word for "thank you" in Sara, so many people have adopted the French *merci*.

Sara also has the interesting feature of having a double plural form—that is, some plural words can be made plural again. For example, *de* means "a person," and *dege* means "people." However, *degege* means "a group of people."

Chad is a land that has a wealth of languages. This means that most people must learn at least a portion of a second language such as French, Arabic, or Sara just to talk to people from other towns or areas. This diversity of languages makes Chad a fascinating place.

COMMON SARA WORDS AND PHRASES:

Hello . . . . Lapia
Goodbye . . . . Aou lapia (literally, "Go well")
Goodbye . . . . Indi lapia (meaning "stay well," the response to aou lapia)
How are you? . . . . I baing?
I'm fine . . . . Mto kari
House . . . . Kei
Food . . . . Yan kessa
Eat . . . . Issa
Drink . . . . Aing
Fire . . . . Por
Friend . . . . Maade
Play . . . . Ndam
Give me water to drink . . . Adoum man maing

INTERNET LINKS

endangeredlanguages.com/lang/country/Chad
This web page from the Endangered Languages Project lists the endangered languages of Chad and provides links to learn more about them.

www.tchad.org/research/language.html
Virtual Chad offers an overview of Chadian languages and links to learn short phrases in Chadian Arabic, Ngambai, and Dadjo.

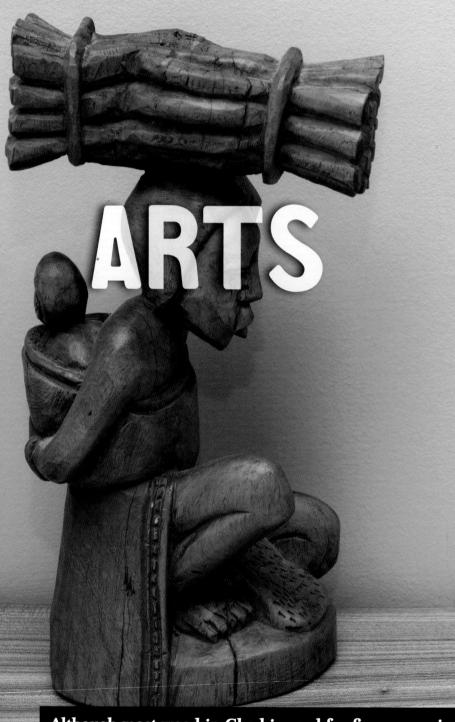

ARTS

Although most wood in Chad is used for fires, some is carved into statues depicting everyday life, such as this one of a woman carrying her child and a bundle of sticks.

10

I N CHAD, MUSIC AND ART ARE PART OF everyday life. Skills such as pottery and weaving are both practical and beautiful, and making music is a popular form of entertainment at gatherings. These traditions go back to ancient times, and although many still practice them in the same ways they have always been done, some people are starting to adapt them to modern life. In particular, old traditions such as storytelling and folklore are finding a new outlet through film. Chad is just beginning to be recognized internationally for all it has to offer the arts.

The most popular places for playing music in Chad are at church, in bars, and at village dance nights.

ART TRADITIONS

More than 80 percent of Chad's population is employed in subsistence farming or herding. Most of these people have little contact with the area outside of their immediate homeland. Their handicrafts, although constantly improving and changing, belong to local traditions that have been in existence for hundreds of years. These arts include woven mats, wood carvings, leather products, jewelry, and wool rugs.

Large pottery is made to store food.

Chadians also make baskets, mats, and fans from straw. One widely practiced craft is that of carving calabashes (a type of gourd). The calabashes are etched with many intricate geometric shapes and used for household purposes or turned into musical instruments.

Potters make items such as clay pots and cups by using coils of clay added one at a time on top of each other. Gradually the pot takes shape under the potter's skillful fingers. After the pots are finished, they must be put into a fire so that they will harden. The potter keeps watch on the fire, and when it is very, very hot, he covers the fire with sand. By morning, the potter will have his wares ready to take to market.

Also, women are adept at embroidery and men at carving leather and wood statues. People also weave tapestries and carve objects from soapstone. They make these items to sell to earn a little money. People take their items to a market, where they are often traded to merchants to sell to others. These merchants often are Arabs, who have been the dominant force in trade in Chad for centuries.

Traditional musical instruments include trumpets made from the horns of goats, a kind of harp called a *kinde*, and a tin horn called a *kakaki*. An instrument that uses calabashes is the *hu hu*. Among the Sara, people use whistles, large drums called *kodjos*, and balafons, which are like xylophones.

The traditional music of the Sara combines flutelike sounds with drums. The music of the Bagirmi people more often combines drums with zithers. Zithers are sound boxes that have 30 to 40 strings and are played with fingers, a bow, or a plucking instrument. The Bagirmi also have a traditional dance that involves the use of grain-pounding pestles, which they pretend to use on the other dancers.

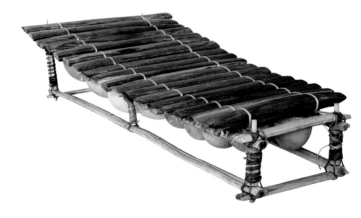

Balafons, such as the one shown here, are made from strips of wood laid over gourds and held together by a bamboo frame. They are played with rubber mallets, and the hollow gourds help to amplify the sound of the wood being struck.

WRITING

Though few Chadians have attained a high level of literacy, several writers of note have come from Chad. Joseph Brahim Seid is a Chadian writer and politician. He wrote books now considered classics in Chad, including *Au Tchad sous les étoiles* (*In Chad Under the Stars*, 1962) and *Un enfant du Tchad* (*A Child of Chad*, 1967), based on his own life. The playwright Baba Moustapha left a posthumous publication, *Le Commandant Chaka* (1983), in which he denounced military dictatorships.

Koulsy Lamko is another writer from Chad. He was born in 1959. His works include a collection of poems, *Aurore* (2001); a play, *Corps et Voix: Paroles Rhizome* (2001); and a novel, *La Phaléne des Collines* (2000). A poet, Nocky Djedanoum, who was also born in 1959, has published a collection of poems on the Rwandan genocide in Nyamirambo, which was presented at the Fest'Africa in 2000. Djedanoum was the director of the Fest'Africa that year.

In addition to stories, people around the world also like to repeat favorite sayings, or proverbs. You may be familar with the saying, "The grass is always greener on the other side," which means that people tend to think that what others have is better than what they have. People in Chad also have favorite sayings.

A few Teda sayings:

Kûdi hi gûshi labannuún.
"Don't let the dog guard the ribs."
Do not put untrustworthy people in charge of something you want to keep safe.

Wûroei nôushi gunu.
"Precaution is not fear."
Preparing for danger is not the same thing as being afraid of it.

Aba murdom yidado, ba murdom yidannó yugó.
"Anyone with 10 fingers has at least 10 relatives."
Everyone has people they can count on.

A few Sara sayings:

Ngon àw mba tá, gèr mba.
"A child first goes on a trip, then discovers a stranger."
If people stay at home, they never learn about others. To learn about other people, you need to travel outside your hometown to meet them.

Áá kä döi tä à, kä ji tä òso.
"If you notice what is on your head, you'll drop what is in your hand."
You cannot pay strict attention to more than one thing at a time.

Gòwró kä ngon ì kä kùmänèé.
"Even a small squash has seeds."
In a meeting, even a child should be able to have a say.

FOLKLORE

Like people around the world, Chadians enjoy telling stories and passing them down from generation to generation. They mix traditional tales with things found in the modern world.

One story explains the behavior of goats, dogs, and sheep. One day, the sheep, the goat, and the dog wanted to travel and waited for a truck to arrive. When a truck came, the driver said it would be 500 francs to go to Sarh. The sheep paid 500 francs, the dog paid 1,000 francs, and the goat asked to pay on arrival. When they arrived in Sarh, the goat ran away without paying, and when the dog asked about his change, the driver replied, "Go ask the goat for your 500 francs." This story explains why dogs chase trucks, goats run from them, and sheep don't move—the sheep has already paid his fee.

Other stories tell people how to live. One is about a monkey who rescued a hyena from a well. After the monkey took the hyena home, the hyena wanted

Animals such as sheep and goats are common in Chadian folktales because they are well-known parts of everyday life.

Local folktales teach young people about their culture and prepare them for success in their community.

to eat him. The monkey evaded the hyena and managed to trick him back down into the well, where the hyena drowned. Such stories with morals—which in this case is, "Don't hurt the people who help you"—teach people how they are expected to behave in society.

FILM

At least two Chadians have become film directors of international renown. They are Issa Serge Coelo and Mahamat-Saleh Haroun. Both now live in Paris.

Issa Serge Coelo was born in N'Djamena in 1967. He studied in Paris but what he really wanted to do was direct films about his home country. His first feature-length film was *Daresalam* (2000). The movie follows two childhood friends, Koni and Djimi, who flee their village after the government soldiers destroy it because the villagers are too poor to pay their taxes. Koni and Djimi join a rebel band, thinking they will be able to transform Chad into a better place and help those who are denied justice. However, as they spend more time with the rebels, they realize the rebels themselves are more interested in power than in helping people.

The director shows this by having both the government officials and the rebel leaders speak to the main characters in French, a language of occupation, rather than in their native tongue. Ultimately, Koni and Djimi come to different conclusions as to how Chad can really be helped and how high the cost is. In the end, the young men find themselves foes on opposite sides, physically disabled and morally at a loss.

In 2001, *Daresalam* was shown at film festivals in Berlin, San Francisco, Moscow, London, and the African Film Festival in New York. Before this movie, Coelo worked on a short film, *Un Taxi pour Aouzou*, which won several awards at film festivals in 1997.

Mahamat-Saleh Haroun was born in Abéché in 1961. He fled Chad during the civil wars, settling first in Cameroon and then in France. At first, he worked as a journalist, but his interest soon turned toward telling stories through film. He made two documentaries in the early 1990s and finished his first feature film, *Bye, Bye Africa*, in 1999. The film won several prizes at international film festivals. His second film, *Abouna* (*Our Father*, 2002), was filmed in Chad and tells the story of two young boys who go looking for their missing father. Haroun cast native Chadians, none of them actors, in his film. He even allowed the child playing the elder brother to choose the boy who would play his younger brother, as he believed that the bond between the children would work better on film if it was already present in real life.

Since then, Haroun has made four other feature films, three in Chad and one in both Chad and France. His movies *Daratt* (*Dry Season*, 2006) and *Un homme qui crie* (*A Screaming Man*, 2010) won him many awards at international film festivals.

Haroun is adamant about making more movies in his home country even though there are hardly any professional actors there, no film technicians, and no resources to fund film production. The director believes that the people of Chad, who usually watch foreign films dubbed in French if they see movies at all, do not identify with the Europeans or Americans they see on the screen. He wants them to see images of themselves and to experience stories that are about their lives and what is important to them.

Watching a movie is a communal experience in Chad. A movie night happens when someone who owns or borrows a television and a generator acquires a movie to show. The people in the household then advertise that they will be showing the movie and will be charging an admission price of a few cents. Adults and children will come to the home, carrying their own chairs or a mat, and watch the movie outdoors on the television when it gets dark. Many of the films seen by Chadians in this way are Japanese kung-fu movies, and some Chadians have seen the few that are available so many times that they can memorize all the dialogue, even though it is in Japanese!

In small villages such as this one, movie nights are rare and special occasions.

INTERNATIONAL ART

Chad is beginning to emerge onto the international stage for the arts. In 2003, the Arts et Medias d'Afrique held its 10-year anniversary celebration in Chad. The arts festival featured more than 100 writers and artists who showcased their work around the theme "Peace And War: What About Commitment?" The aim was to review African literature of the 20th century, to discuss the state of artistic production and the place of writers and artists during times of peace, and to strengthen artistic ties between Africa and the West Indies.

Other topics, such as HIV/AIDS and its impact on Africa, were also discussed. The festival also featured a carnival to mobilize local talent in N'Djamena, an outdoor cinema, and concerts involving musicians from Chad.

INTERNET LINKS

www.tchad.org/research/art.html
Virtual Chad provides an introduction to art in Chad. The website also offers pages on literature, folklore, and proverbs.

LEISURE

Although an internet connection is hard to come by outside of N'Djamena, smartphones and tablets are used to take pictures and listen to music or the Quran.

11

LEISURE TIME IS A LUXURY WHEN there are animals to be herded, crops to tend to, and families to provide for. Most Chadians have little time or money for activities such as going to the movies or watching television. Many of them live without electricity, so they have no computers, telephones, or electronic games. However, that does not mean no one in Chad ever has any fun!

There are only 3 television channels in Chad, but there are more than 40 radio stations.

Most households have battery-operated radios, and some have a cassette player or CD player. Some people who live near the capital city even have smartphones. Most adults have bicycles to ride, although most children do not. Sports are popular, as is spending time with friends and family at night when little work can be done.

PLAYING SPORTS

Chadians are very fond of sports. One of their favorites is soccer, which is called football in Chad. The country sponsors a national soccer team that competes internationally.

Chad's best athletes are young men who may have often faced hunger, childhood diseases, and other hardships that athletes from most other nations have never had to face. As a result, they may not be as large and strong as soccer players from other nations. However, that does not mean

Village life is often difficult without access to electricity or running water, but people find many ways to entertain themselves.

they do not love the game as much as other soccer players do.

Teams from wealthier countries can get companies to sponsor them and can afford to hire the best trainers and coaches. Chad's national soccer team does not have many of these resources.

In September 2019, Chad was defeated 3—1 by Sudan's team to qualify for the 2022 FIFA World Cup. After nearly 30 years on the circuit, the Chadian team has yet to win a match when it comes time to qualify for the World Cup or the Africa Cup of Nations. However, nearly everyone in Chad follows the team's accomplishments on the radio. Even if their team does not win, people are eager to listen to the games and want to know how their players are doing.

In the cities, boys play basketball as well as soccer. They also play handball and participate in track and field activities. Schools organize their own sports teams, as do some companies. Local sports teams will play against one another throughout the year. High schools choose their best players to enter the annual Semaine Culturelle Sportive, which is a national sporting competition.

VILLAGE LIFE

On Sundays and market days in the south, people gather for dancing and enjoy *bili-bili*, a beer derived from millet. People in N'Djamena will also visit the cinema, restaurants, or open-air bars to relax and talk with their friends. Men will play cards or checkers, while women braid each other's hair or embroider. In the villages, people enjoy storytelling, drumming, and dancing in the evening, while in the cities, they visit dance clubs and bars. Still, because acquiring enough food to eat is a problem for many, most people in Chad do not have a lot of leisure time, especially in the small towns and villages.

CAMEL RACING

Throughout the Sahara, camel racing is a popular sport for social gatherings and festivals. Although most Westerners imagine camels leisurely bumping through the sand, they are capable of sustaining a running speed of 25 miles (40 km) per hour. For short bursts, they can run up to 40 miles (64 km) per hour.

Near the Tibesti Massif, the Toubou people organize some of the best camel races in the country. The area is known for its chasms and cliffs, making the races challenging and exciting. Although non-Muslims are not allowed to enter these races, they are sometimes able to watch the spectacle from afar.

Camels are hardy animals native to the Sahara. Humans first began to ride them more than 5,000 years ago.

Most Chadian children make their own toys and amuse themselves with whatever they can find. They will create things from wire, clay, or tin cans. When boys play soccer, they are usually barefoot and will use a ball made of rags bound together or formed from plastic bags. Girls will play with dolls, jump ropes, and jacks (using stones instead of metal jacks), as well as games that involve clapping. Both boys and girls enjoy playing hide-and-seek.

Other popular games include bocce ball, a lawn game played with one target ball (the pallina) and eight larger "bocce" balls for scoring, and mancala, a two-person game that involves moving handfuls of small tokens around a board in the hopes of collecting the most. People of all ages enjoy these games.

Children enjoy hoop racing down the streets of N'Djamena.

Elderly people are still needed to work in the fields and care for the animals. Older children sacrifice whatever free time they may have in order to sell peanuts, mangoes, eggs, or soap in the market to make a little money.

Chad may be a poor country and the people hardworking, but they still find the time to relax with their friends and family after a hard day's work. Just like other people around the world, family and friends are very important to Chadians. They enjoy having the chance to sing or dance together. Women like to embroider, knit, or crochet. This sort of activity is enjoyable but also produces goods the women can sell at the market to help their family.

Near the Cameroon border, children play in the Chari River.

Childhood is usually short in Chad, with children being given more and more responsibility as they get older. Children often have to make their own toys and invent their own games. Adults and children alike nonetheless find the time to chat, braid hair, or play soccer. Life in Chad is often difficult, but people have fun whenever they can.

INTERNET LINKS

www.backyardbocce.com/basic-rules
This resource explains how to play bocce ball.

gathertogethergames.com/mancala
This web page includes simple instructions and a tutorial video on how to play mancala.

www.topendsports.com/world/countries/chad.htm
This web page gives an overview of sports in Chad.

FESTIVALS

Camel races are a popular activity at festivals in Chad. Sometimes up to 200 camels will race at once.

12

C HADIANS CELEBRATE MANY holidays—Christian, Muslim, and secular alike. Chad has 12 public holidays: New Year's Day (January 1), International Women's Day (March 8), Easter (March or April), Labour Day (May 1), Independence Day (August 11), All Saints' Day (November 1), Republic Day (November 28), Freedom and Democracy Day (December 1), and Christmas (December 25), as well as Eid al-Fitr (the end of Ramadan), Eid al-Adha (the Feast of the Sacrifice), and Mawlid (the Prophet's Birthday), which are celebrated according to the Islamic calendar.

MUSLIM HOLIDAYS

HAJJ One of the most important things a Muslim is supposed to do is complete a pilgrimage to Mecca, in Saudi Arabia, but only if they have the financial means to do so. This pilgrimage is called the hajj. The annual hajj season occurs near the end of the year, during the month of Dhu al-Hijjah. Every year, up to 4 million people travel to Mecca to participate in this

observance. The pilgrims include Muslims from many countries, including Chad.

Before the trip, the pilgrim is required to dress in special clothes called *ihram*. These clothes are made of two sheets of white unhemmed cloth and include sandals. By wearing the same clothing, the pilgrims, regardless of their wealth or social standing, show their equality with one another.

Once the pilgrim arrives in Mecca, they must circle the Kaaba seven times in a counterclockwise direction. The Kaaba is a shrine that is the most sacred location in Islam. After circling the Kaaba, the pilgrim

The Kaaba stands in the middle of the Grand Mosque in Saudi Arabia.

walks between the hills of Safa and Marwa seven times. This completes the "lesser hajj," or *umrah*. The pilgrim can now go home or continue with the "greater hajj," or Al Hajjul Akbar.

To complete the greater hajj, the pilgrim must do three more things. They must go to the hill of Arafat and spend an afternoon there. The time spent at Arafat is usually devoted to prayer and contemplation. After this, the pilgrim goes to the city of Mina, where they collect stones to throw at three pillars that represent the devil. After stoning the devil, the pilgrim walks around the Kaaba seven more times. A pilgrim who has completed the hajj may attach the title al-Hajj or Hajji (Pilgrim) to his name (for female pilgrims, it is Hajjah).

One of the most important feasts on the Islamic calendar happens at the end of the hajj season. It is Eid al-Adha.

EID AL-ADHA In Chad, Eid al-Adha, or the Feast of the Sacrifice, is sometimes known as Tabaski. It takes place on the 10th day of Dhu al-Hijjah at the end of the hajj season. Celebrating Tabaski shows a Muslim's commitment, obedience, and devotion to Allah. According to the Quran, Allah asked Abraham (Ibrahim in Arabic) to sacrifice his son, and when Abraham took his son Ishmael to the place of sacrifice, Allah provided a sheep to be sacrificed instead. In memory

The Islamic calendar, or the Hijri, is based on the phases of the moon. Each month begins with the sighting of the first crescent moon, which usually appears a day or so after the new moon. The year is 12 months long, but because it is based on the moon rather than the sun, it is not the same length as the Gregorian year, which runs from January 1 to December 31. The Hijri is 11 days shorter than the Gregorian calendar.

The actual beginning of each month is difficult to predict in advance, since the months do not change until the crescent moon is sighted by Muslim authorities. Therefore, each month can have either 29 or 30 days.

The 12 months of the calendar are:

Muharram
Rajab
Safar
Sha'ban
Rabi al-Awwal
Ramadan
Rabi al-Thani
Shawwal
Jumada al-Awwal
Dhu al-Qi'dah
Jumada al-Thani
Dhu al-Hijjah

The seven days of the week are:

Al-ahad (Sunday)
Al-ithnayn (Monday)
Al-thalatha (Tuesday)
Al-arba'a (Wednesday)
Al-khamis (Thursday)
Al-jumu'ah (Friday)
As-sabt (Saturday)

of this, many Muslims will sacrifice a sheep on Tabaski. Families who do not have sheep may sacrifice a goat or some other animal. The family who owned the sacrificed animal keeps only one-third of the meat and distributes the rest to other family members, friends, and the poor. Because of this custom, many people who are too poor to afford meat are able to eat it at this time of the year.

Tabaski lasts several days. During this time, people socialize with their friends and family, and everyone enjoys special meals of favorite dishes and wonderful desserts. Sometimes children are presented with gifts and sweets to mark the festival.

In Christian and Jewish traditions, it is Isaac, not Ishmael, whom Abraham is asked to sacrifice.

RAMADAN AND EID AL-FITR   Another way in which Muslims show their devotion to Allah is to fast from sunrise to sundown during Ramadan, the ninth month of the Islamic calendar.

At the end of Ramadan, Muslims enjoy the three-day festival called Eid al-Fitr, which celebrates the good things Allah has given them. During Ramadan, Muslims may pay a voluntary tax in food or money that is given to the poor so that they can celebrate Eid al-Fitr with everyone else.

Many people who have the resources put up decorations in their homes during Eid al-Fitr, and everyone who can afford it will have new clothes to wear. People go to special early-morning prayers in large open areas or mosques. Although Muslims are supposed to pray every morning, special prayers are offered during Eid al-Fitr.

Celebrations begin after everyone gets home from prayer. Children may be given small amounts of money. People begin visiting one another around mid-morning, and at each stop they eat special cakes. Since people want to

Many goats are brought to market during Eid al-Fitr to feed everyone while they celebrate.

visit many extended family and friends, the visits are very short. The occasion is very joyous, and everyone visits as many people as they can.

Dinner is spent with family, and then everyone goes visiting again in the evenings. The streets are full of music, dancing, fireworks, and games to celebrate this important festival. By the end of the holiday, both the children and the adults are exhausted from all the preparations, eating, and visiting. Eid al-Fitr is one of the highlights of the Muslim year. Even if a family cannot afford to give gifts of money or to decorate their home, the celebratory spirit of spending their time together and cooking with their friends and family members makes Eid al-Fitr a festive time.

CHRISTIAN OBSERVANCES

CHRISTMAS   Christmas is celebrated a bit differently in Chad than in the United States. People do not put up Christmas trees, and Santa Claus is not a popular part of the holiday. Many people are too poor to buy toys for their children, and most of them probably do not live near a store that sells toys in any case. However, Chadians still enjoy the Christmas season very much.

What is important about Christmas in Chad is the spiritual part of the holiday. People celebrate by visiting one another, sharing special meals, and being thankful for their family and friends. Artists may paint nativity scenes. Since many people do not have electricity, they will not have Christmas lights, but they may put up garland or other homemade decorations.

Choirs perform Christmas songs at gatherings, and people sing Christmas carols as they do in the United States. Instead of turkey or ham, people will eat goat or sheep. They attend church services on Christmas Eve, and everyone looks forward to spending an entire day with their family the next day.

EASTER   The season of Lent is the most somber time in the Christian calendar, since it is the season leading up to the commemoration of the death and resurrection of Jesus Christ. Churches will conduct special services, including services on Ash Wednesday, Maundy Thursday, and Good Friday. The most joyful celebration comes on Easter Sunday, when Christians go to church to celebrate Jesus's resurrection from the dead. At church, they sing songs of joy, sometimes accompanied by drums or other instruments.

At Easter, some Catholic churches perform mass baptisms. All the people who are to be baptized dress in white, and after Mass everyone goes from the church to the home of each newly baptized person. If 20 people have been baptized, then the whole church ends up at 20 different houses. At each home, people eat and sing hymns. They also sing while walking from home to home.

After church services, people gather with their families to eat Easter meals. If they have a job in the city, they will have the Monday after Easter off to stay home with their family as well.

SECULAR CELEBRATIONS

Africa Day on May 25 commemorates the founding of the Organization of African Unity in Addis Ababa, Ethiopia. Many African nations observe Africa Day as a holiday. In Chad, some people celebrate Africa Day with contests, sports, and dances. On Independence Day, August 11, Chadians mark the anniversary of their independence with speeches and flag-raising ceremonies.

On holidays, people decorate the streets by painting tree trunks white and hanging flags and banners everywhere. Holidays recognized by the government are often celebrated with parades that feature people performing native dances. Important people in the government will make speeches. The parades, speeches, and decorations are indicators of the celebratory spirit.

Another date celebrated in Chad is International Women's Day on March 8. Although it is not considered a holiday in the United States, it is one of the main holidays in Chad. On this day, women form their own parades, race bicycles, and participate in soccer matches. In a festive spirit of celebration, men dress as women and serve food to the women, who are dressed as men.

Every year, a new fabric is designed to honor International Women's Day, and women across the country buy this fabric to design their holiday outfit. Thus, women from all corners of the country will be wearing the same fabric on this day. International Women's Day is also the one day of the year when most women will go to bars and restaurants.

A common practice of some young people in the capital is called *pari-vente*. A young woman, or a group of young women, will rent a bar for the day and sell alcohol, hoping to make a profit. They will invite all their friends and family to participate, but others are also welcomed. Although the government does not approve of this custom, it is still practiced in the non-Muslim parts of N'Djamena.

Festivals in Chad are celebrated for both religious and secular reasons and are wonderful opportunities for friends and family to get together and eat delicious meals. Like other people around the world, Chadians consider their families to be very important and appreciate the time they can spend with their loved ones during these special celebrations every year.

On Independence Day in 2020, President Déby was awarded the title of Field Marshal of Chad for his efforts against terrorism.

FOOD

Most cooking in Chad is done in large pots over open wood fires, such as this one at a camp in the Sahara.

13

T HE FOOD IN CHAD IS TYPICAL OF the Saharan region, involving grains, vegetables, and meats that are locally available. Most people are isolated or on the nomadic move, so supply chains from other countries or even from other parts of Chad are almost nonexistent. Agricultural products such as millet, sorghum, and peanuts are common, as are okra, cassava leaves, and sweet potatoes. Stews and sauces are popular because they are easy to prepare over wood fires, help stretch out food reserves, and can feed many people at once.

Food is very important to Chadians as a part of socializing. Eating is a communal activity in Chad, and no one wants to eat alone. If a person is going to be alone for a meal, they will either visit friends and family or invite someone over.

COMMON DISHES

Peanuts (called groundnuts in Chad) are one of the most important elements of the Chadian diet, along with sorghum and millet. Most of the peanuts grown are consumed locally, with only 3 to 5 percent sold to mills. People use raw peanuts and peanut butter in many of their recipes.

Many people in Chad eat fish, but due to the lack of refrigeration and transportation, it is usually dried or smoked before being sold at the

Fishing in Chad's
lakes and rivers is
generally done in
traditional boats
such as
this pirogue.

Though we think of
the peanut as a nut,
it is really a legume
and thus closely
related to the pea.

markets. Banda is a popular smoked fish cut into segments and exported to Nigeria, Cameroon, and the Central African Republic. The Hausa, Kotoko, and Bornuan ethnic groups commonly prepare it. Nile perch, called capitaine in Chad, is a fish that weighs more than 100 pounds (45 kilograms). It is often exported to Europe, though many people in Chad also like to eat it. At the beginning of the rainy season, people go fishing for balbout, a kind of catfish.

The most common meat Chadians eat is goat. Beef is served on some occasions, but most cattle are used for milk production and are not slaughtered. When beef is eaten, most Chadians can only afford to give each person in the family two or three bites.

Milk is sometimes heated and mixed with sugar, or it is turned into yogurt or butter. Fruits such as guavas, bananas, and mangoes are available seasonally, especially in the south. In the north, people like to eat dates. Rice and pasta are less commonly served compared to millet, and a family will reserve them for special occasions.

Millet is a grain that is not usually eaten by people in the United States. Most people in the United States are probably more familiar with millet as an ingredient in birdseed. The small, white and red spherical seeds in birdseed mixtures are millet seeds.

In some parts of the world, millet is an important grain that people eat nearly every day. Millet matures rapidly, so it will grow even in very short growing seasons. It is tolerant of dry climates and poor soil conditions. It can also be stored for a long time, so people can keep stocks of millet in case of famine.

Today, people grow more than 6,000 varieties of millet across the world. Many of these are grown to be fed only to animals. The ones most often consumed by people are pearl millet, finger millet, golden millet, fox-tail millet, Japanese millet, Teff millet, and ditch millet.

Baked millet balls, or *aiyash*, are a staple of the Chadian diet and are served with flavorful sauces that reflect the local culture.

The national dish of Chad is *boule*, and many Chadians eat it almost every day. Boule is a kind of porridge most commonly made of millet (in the south) or corn (in the north), shaped into a ball, and dipped into sauce. Cassava, rice, or sorghum can also be used to make boule. Chadians eat a variety of sauces with their boule, though the basic ingredients of okra, garlic, red pepper, dried tomato flour, and bouillon are included in most of them. In the north, sauces tend to be spicier and have more meat in them. One of these northern sauces is called *nashif*, and it is made with spicy tomato sauce and chopped beef.

Another common dish is *bouillie*, which is made from millet and peanuts and is flavored with lemon and sometimes sugar. The result is a milky porridge that is drunk either cold or warm. It is usually served as a breakfast dish but may be served at dinner as well. It is one of the special foods fed to pregnant women, children, and people who are sick, much like chicken soup is in the United States.

Many women will make their own beer, which is called bili-bili. Its basic ingredient is millet. Beer is popular with many southern Chadians. The town of Moundou is the home of the Gala Brewery, which produces more than a million barrels of beer annually. The brewery remained in operation even during Chad's civil wars and droughts. Beer is rarely available in the north, since Muslims do not consume alcohol. Chadians also enjoy cola, and some people make a type of fruit juice from the hibiscus plant, which they bottle at home. Everyone drinks tea sweetened with lots of sugar.

EATING IN CHAD

In Chad, many people do not eat breakfast, and those who do often simply eat leftovers from the day before. The main meal of the day is eaten at midday, and a smaller meal is eaten near sundown. Women usually do all the cooking over open fires. In many areas of Chad, women and children eat in a separate area from the men.

Chadians usually sit outdoors on mats to eat around a large common bowl. People will begin eating only after the host has prayed or indicated that everyone can start the meal. It is considered rude for a guest to refuse food, and when a guest stops eating, everyone else will also stop and consider their meal finished.

People do not like to eat in public as this is considered rude. To accommodate this, the interior of restaurants are hidden behind straw fences so that they cannot be seen from the street. Other conventions concerning food include limiting what a pregnant woman may consume so that her baby will not be too big to deliver and refusing to give eggs to children lest they grow up to become thieves. Also, most people eat only with the right hand, which is a Muslim custom even non-Muslims follow.

For holidays, Chadians eat a special stew called *marrara*. It is made from the intestines, stomach, liver, and kidneys of a goat and is considered a delicacy. In Chad, guests are always welcome, as hospitality is considered very important. A guest will always be offered refreshment, even if it is only a glass of water and a place to sit in the shade. If guests arrive near mealtime, they will be invited to join the family. Women customarily prepare enough food for the family and a guest or two, just in case a friend or a neighbor drops by. No matter how little a family has, they will offer to share their food.

INTERNET LINKS

www.internationalcuisine.com/about-food-and-culture-of-chad
This blog post includes links to Chadian recipes.

traveltips.usatoday.com/food-chad-africa-17229.html
This article from *USA Today* offers an overview of common foods in Chad.

MAHARAGWE (RED BEANS IN COCONUT SAUCE)

1 cup dried red kidney beans

2 chopped onions

1 tablespoon oil

2 or 3 chopped tomatoes

1 teaspoon salt

2 teaspoons turmeric

3 ground chili peppers or 1 ½ teaspoons cayenne pepper

2 cups (0.5 liters) coconut milk

In a large pot, cover the kidney beans with water, and simmer for about one hour. Cook the chopped onions in oil until golden brown. Add onions and remaining ingredients to the pot with the beans, and simmer about 20 minutes. Serve over rice or other grains.

DARABA (SWEET POTATO AND OKRA STEW)

20 chopped okra

3 chopped tomatoes

1 cup shredded mixed greens

1 cubed sweet potato

1 cubed eggplant

¾ cup peanut butter

1 bouillon cube, any flavor

Salt, pepper, and cayenne pepper to taste

Add vegetables to a pot, and cover with water and spices. Bring water to a boil, and then reduce heat, simmering for 30 minutes. Remove ¾ cup (177 milliliters) of the liquid from the pot, and mix with the peanut butter until smooth. Add the peanut butter mixture and the bouillon cube to the vegetables, and simmer another 10 minutes, until the sauce has thickened. Serve over rice or other grains.

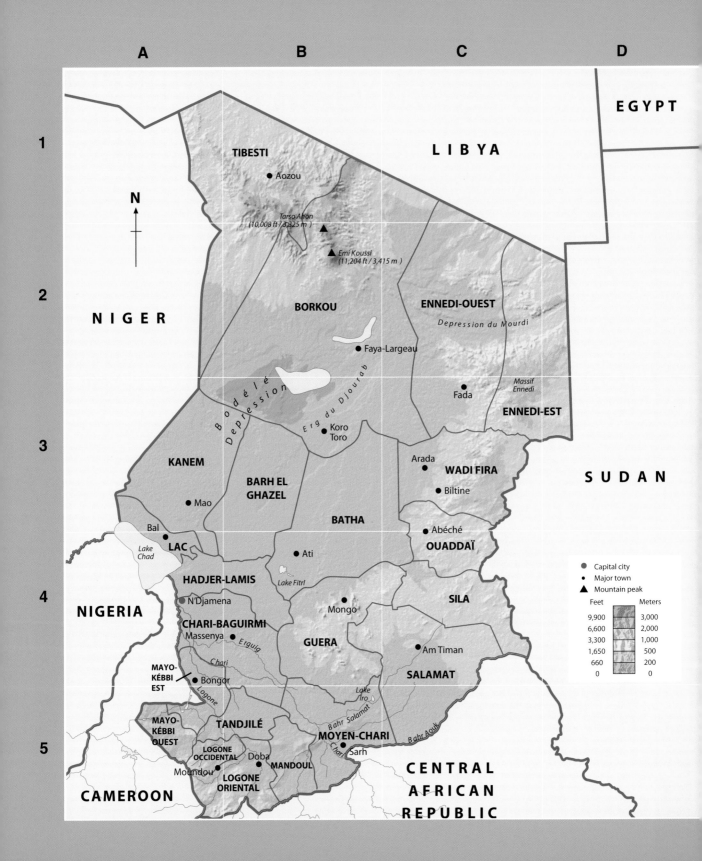

MAP OF CHAD

ECONOMIC CHAD

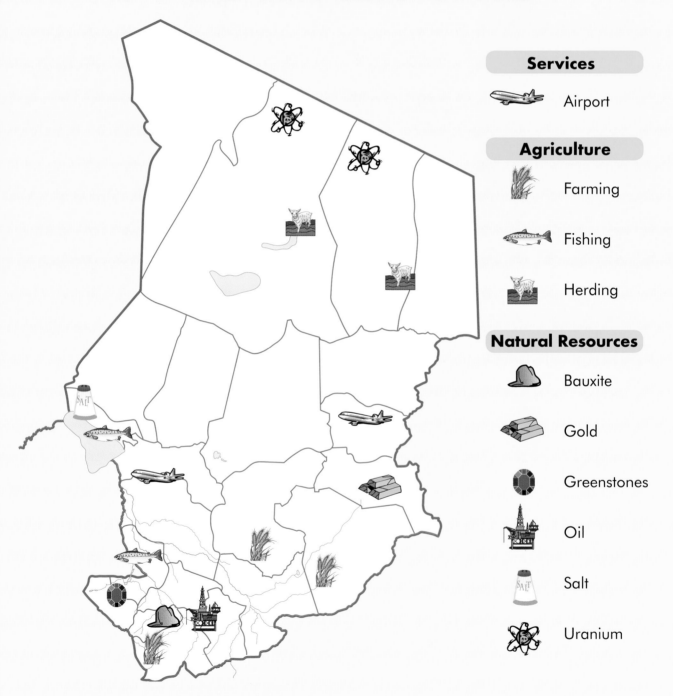

Services

Airport

Agriculture

Farming

Fishing

Herding

Natural Resources

Bauxite

Gold

Greenstones

Oil

Salt

Uranium

ABOUT THE ECONOMY

All figures are 2017 estimates unless otherwise noted.

GROSS DOMESTIC PRODUCT (GDP)
$26.46 billion (2019)

GDP BY SECTOR
agriculture 52.3 percent, industry 14.7 percent, services 33.1 percent

POPULATION BELOW POVERTY LINE
46.7 percent (2011)

TOURISM
approximately 100,000 tourists per year

INFLATION
-0.9 percent

WORKFORCE
more than 80 percent involved in subsistence farming or herding

CURRENCY
Central African CFA franc (XAF)—responsible authority is the Bank of the Central African States
1 USD (U.S. dollar) = 538 XAF (December 2020)
coins: 1, 5, 10, 25, 50, 100, 500 francs;
notes: 500, 1,000, 2,000, 5,000, 10,000 francs

AGRICULTURAL PRODUCTS
cotton, sorghum, millet, peanuts, rice, potatoes, cassava

MAJOR EXPORTS
oil, cotton, cattle, gum arabic

IMPORTS
machinery, industrial goods, petroleum products, textiles, foodstuffs

MAJOR TRADING PARTNERS
France, United States, China, Cameroon, Netherlands

CULTURAL CHAD

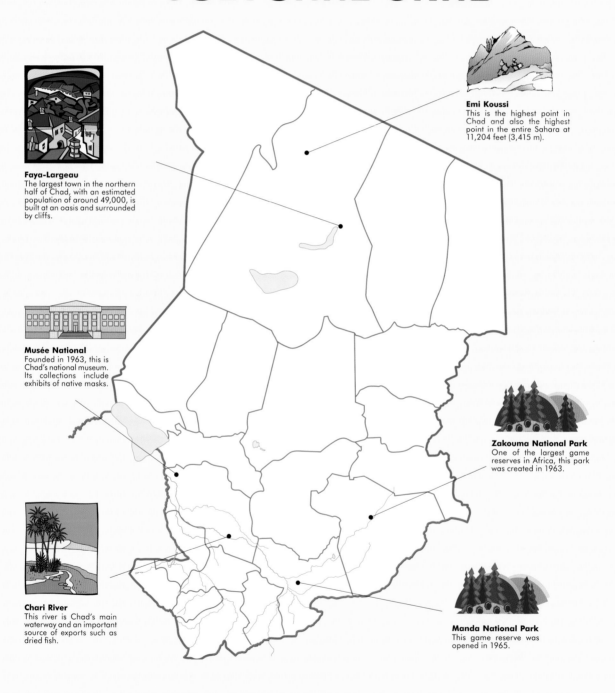

Emi Koussi
This is the highest point in Chad and also the highest point in the entire Sahara at 11,204 feet (3,415 m).

Faya-Largeau
The largest town in the northern half of Chad, with an estimated population of around 49,000, is built at an oasis and surrounded by cliffs.

Musée National
Founded in 1963, this is Chad's national museum. Its collections include exhibits of native masks.

Zakouma National Park
One of the largest game reserves in Africa, this park was created in 1963.

Chari River
This river is Chad's main waterway and an important source of exports such as dried fish.

Manda National Park
This game reserve was opened in 1965.

ABOUT THE CULTURE

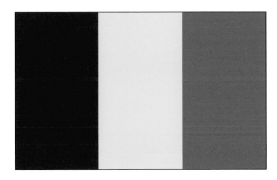

All figures are 2020 estimates unless otherwise noted.

OFFICIAL NAME
Republic of Chad

FLAG
three equal vertical bands with blue on the hoist side, then yellow and red; design was based on the flag of France

CAPITAL
N'Djamena

OTHER MAJOR CITIES
Moundou, Sarh, Abéché

POPULATION
16.9 million

ETHNIC GROUPS
more than 200 distinct groups;
in the north: Arabs, Gorane, Zaghawa, Kanembou, Ouaddai, Bagirmi, Hadjerai, Fulani, Kotoko, Hausa, Boulala, Maba
in the south: Sara, Moundang, Moussei, Massa

LIFE EXPECTANCY
58.3 years

MAJOR RELIGIONS
Muslim 52.1 percent, Christian 44.1 percent, animist 0.3 percent, other 3.5 percent

OFFICIAL LANGUAGES
French and Arabic

LITERACY RATE
22.3 percent

IMPORTANT ANNIVERSARY
Independence Day (August 11)

TIMELINE

IN CHAD	IN THE WORLD
	1530 The beginning of the transatlantic slave trade is organized by the Portuguese in Africa.
	1558–1603 The reign of Elizabeth I of England occurs.
1570–1617 Alooma is king of the Kanem-Bornu kingdom in the region of Chad.	**1620** Pilgrims sail the *Mayflower* to America.
	1776 The U.S. Declaration of Independence is written.
1808 The capital of the Kanem-Bornu kingdom is ravaged by the Fulani.	**1789–1799** The French Revolution takes place.
	1861 The American Civil War begins.
1900 Chad becomes a French colony after the Battle of Kousséri.	**1869** The Suez Canal is opened.
	1914 World War I begins.
	1939 World War II begins.
	1945 The United States drops atomic bombs on Hiroshima and Nagasaki, Japan.
1959 The Republic of Chad is formed.	**1949** The North Atlantic Treaty Organization (NATO) is formed.
1960 The proclamation of Chad's independence becomes official.	
1968 The Cultural Revolution plan is enacted.	**1966–1969** The Chinese Cultural Revolution takes place.
1975 Francois Tombalbaye is assassinated.	
1978 Hissène Habré becomes Chad's premier.	
1980 Civil war breaks out. Almost all of N'Djamena's inhabitants flee to Cameroon.	

IN CHAD	IN THE WORLD
1984	
France and Libya agree on the terms of Libyan withdrawal from Chad.	**1986** A nuclear power disaster occurs at Chernobyl in Ukraine.
1989 The Chad–Libya peace accord is signed.	
1990 Idriss Déby becomes the president of Chad.	**1991** The breakup of the Soviet Union occurs.
1994 The International Court of Justice confirms that Chad, not Libya, has sovereignty over the Aouzou strip. Libyan troops leave the Aouzou strip.	
1996 Idriss Déby wins the presidental election.	**1997** Hong Kong is returned to China.
2001 Idriss Déby is re-elected president.	**2001** Terrorists crash planes in New York, Washington, D.C., and Pennsylvania.
2004 Chad receives the first oil payments from the Chad–Cameroon pipeline project.	**2003** The Iraq War begins.
2006 Idriss Déby wins the presidential election.	**2008** Barack Obama is elected the United States' first African American president.
2010 Drought in the Sahel region causes widespread food shortages.	
2011 Idriss Déby wins the presidential election.	**2011** The United States officially declares an end to the Iraq War.
2013 Hissène Habré is arrested in Senegal.	
2016 Idriss Déby wins the presidential election. Hissène Habré is sentenced to life in prison.	**2016** Donald Trump is elected president of the United States.
2018 A new constitution is passed.	**2018** Miguel Diaz-Canel is elected president of Cuba after nearly 60 years of the Castro family's rule.
2020 The death penalty is abolished.	**2020** The COVID-19 pandemic spreads around the world.

GLOSSARY

bili-bili
Homemade beer, typically made by women, derived from millet.

boule
The staple food of Chad, usually made of millet.

groundnuts
The term for peanuts in Chad.

hajj
The pilgrimage to Mecca that all Muslims should make at least once in their lives if they can afford it.

kashimbet
The family unit in Arab culture.

marrara
A special holiday meal made from the internal organs of a goat.

nashif
A spicy northern Chadian sauce that contains beef.

noi
A caste among the Sara who perform priestly functions.

pari-vente
An all-day fundraising event hosted by women selling alcohol.

polders
A series of dikes and periodically flooded fields along the northern end of Lake Chad.

shaykh
The oldest man in an Arab family and the head of the household.

yondo
A Sara initiation rite for young men that was revived during Tombalbaye's cultural revolution.

FOR FURTHER INFORMATION

BOOKS

Collelo, Thomas, ed. *Chad, a Country Study*. Washington, D.C.: U.S. Government Printing Office, 1990.

Debos, Marielle. *Living by the Gun in Chad: Combatants, Impunity and State Formation*. London, UK: Zed Books, 2016.

Toïngar, Esaïe. *A Teenager in the Chad Civil War: A Memoir of Survival, 1982—1986*. Jefferson, NC: McFarland, 2006.

WEBSITES

CIA. *The World Factbook*. "Chad." www.cia.gov/library/publications/the-world-factbook/geos/cd.html.

Human Rights Watch. "Chad." www.hrw.org/africa/chad.

Lonely Planet World Guide. "Chad." www.lonelyplanet.com/chad.

FILMS

Bye, Bye Africa. California Newsreel, 1999.

Daresalam. Arte, 2000.

People and Places of Africa: Chad. Powersports Productions, 1998.

BIBLIOGRAPHY

"Chad Corruption Report." Gan Integrity, updated April 2020. www.ganintegrity.com/portal/country-profiles/chad.

"Chadians." Countries and Their Cultures, accessed November 19, 2020. www.everyculture.com/wc/Brazil-to-Congo-Republic-of/Chadians.html.

"Chad—Mining, Quarrying, and Oil and Gas Exploration." International Trade Administration, accessed November 19, 2020. www.privacyshield.gov/article?id=Chad-Mining-Quarrying-and-Oil-and-Gas-Exploration.

"Chad National Adaptation Plan." United Nations Development Programme, accessed November 19, 2020. www.adaptation-undp.org/projects/chad-national-adaptation-plan.

Dalby, Andrew. *Dictionary of Languages*. New York, NY: Columbia University Press, 2004.

Dugger, Celia W. "World Bank Suspends Loans to Chad Over Use of Oil Money." *New York Times*, January 7, 2006. www.nytimes.com/2006/01/07/politics/world-bank-suspends-loans-to-chad-over-use-of-oil-money.html.

Jones, Douglas Henry. "Chad." *Encyclopaedia Britannica*, updated September 12, 2020. www.britannica.com/place/Chad.

Mays, Terry M. *Africa's First Peacekeeping Operation: The OAU in Chad, 1981—1982*. Westport, CT: Praeger Publishers, 2002.

Riesman, Paul. *Freedom in Fulani Social Life*. Chicago, IL: University of Chicago Press, 1977.

Virtual Chad. www.tchad.org/enhome.html.

INDEX

INDEX